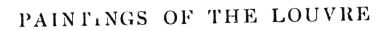

PAINTINGS OF THE LOUVRE

Monna Lisa (No. 1601) Salle IV by da Vinci

Paintings of the Louvre

Italian and Spanish

By
Dr. Arthur Mahler

IN COLLABORATION WITH

Carlos Blacker
and
W. A. Slater

NEW YORK

DOUBLEDAY, PAGE & CO.

1905

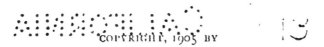

Dedicated to
Solomon Reinach

CONTENTS

LIST OF ILLUSTRATIONS

PAINTINGS OF THE LOUVRE

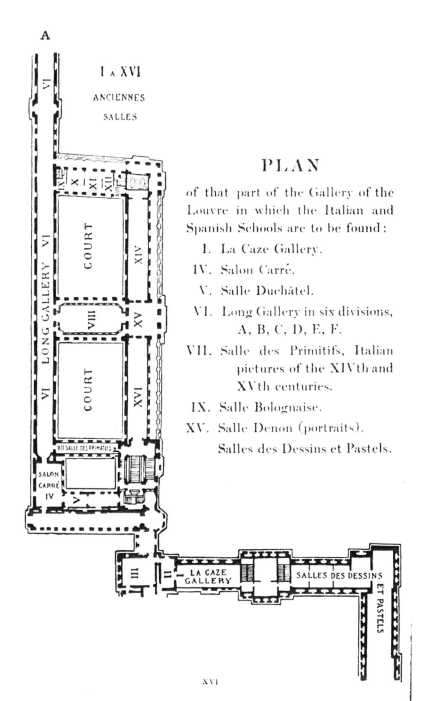

A

I ᴀ XVI

ANCIENNES

SALLES

VI

COURT

VI LONG GALLERY VI

XIV

VIII

XV

COURT

XVI

VII SALLE DES PRIMATIFS

SALON
CARRÉ
IV

V

X XI XII XIII XIV

III II LA CAZE
GALLERY

SALLES DES DESSINS

ET PASTELS

XVI

PLAN

of that part of the Gallery of the
Louvre in which the Italian and
Spanish Schools are to be found:

   I. La Caze Gallery.

  IV. Salon Carré.

   V. Salle Duchâtel.

  VI. Long Gallery in six divisions,
        A, B, C, D, E, F.

 VII. Salle des Primitifs, Italian
        pictures of the XIVth and
        XVth centuries.

  IX. Salle Bolognaise.

  XV. Salle Denon (portraits).

       Salles des Dessins et Pastels.

PAINTINGS OF THE LOUVRE

INTRODUCTION

THE visitor who passes from the lower to the upper galleries of the Louvre might, with reason, be tempted to ask himself where the art of the intervening thousand years was to be found, and, on realizing that his search would be in vain, he might speculate as to the cause or causes which had conspired to make this so.

How and why, he might ask himself, did that perfect art of Greece and its humble Roman imitation find no followers? How and why did they so vanish that art had to be born again and reappear in the form of almost childish attempts at expression a thousand years later?

To these questions, the answer must be that the principal factors in operation were Christianity and Barbarian invasions. Christianity would not, and the Barbarian could not, appreciate those peerless productions which were before their eyes. In them Christianity saw Paganism, and the Barbarian deemed them effeminate and futile.

Rome, the centre of civilization, invaded by wild hordes from without and disintegrated by the new Christian teaching from within, was so radically transformed that the art of the past could find no place in its organism. Olympus was no more, and the representations of its Gods were looked on as impure and idolatrous objects. The temples were abandoned, and many a work of

incomparable beauty was doomed to perish in the fire of
lime-kilns

Then artistic efforts found refuge in the adornment of
objects of daily use, such as sarcophagi, and this, later,
became stereotyped into those Byzantine productions
which still live in the form of religious pictures so called,
while mosaic was much used in decoration. The Byzantine model was the artistic standard and, in this form, Art
lived through the Dark Ages. Gold ornamentation, crude
coloring and rigidity alone prevailed, and the iconoclasts
did the rest. Architecture indeed lived, but it expressed
itself in massiveness rather than beauty. Efforts and
labour were not wanting, but research was trammelled,
and so the results were poor. Then, and only when the
very memory of the great men and great things of the past
seemed to be forgotten for ever, appeared the first glim-
mer of that wonderful light, the Italian Renaissance,
and among the first to herald its dawn was Giovanni
Cimabue.

NOTE

IT will be found that the pictures are given in the order of their numbers. In many cases, the dates of the artists do not agree with those on the pictures, but, where these do not agree, it is because the dates here given are taken from later authorities. In most cases we have given the artists to whom the pictures are attributed on the pictures; but it will be noticed that, in the text, we do not always agree with these authorities. In some catalogues, many more pictures are mentioned, but this is because they give all the pictures that are in the possession of the Louvre, although some of them are in storage. We have tried to give only those that are exhibited and to omit none of these.

This book only deals with the Italian and Spanish Schools, but it is the intention of the authors to treat the other schools of paintings after the same manner in subsequent volumes.

CIMABUE TO FRA ANGELICO

WITH Cimabue (1240–1302), after an eclipse of a thousand years, art finally emerged from darkness. Not that Cimabue was the first to paint on a flat surface with colour, for, even earlier in the thirteenth century, there had been a street in Florence called dei Pittori (of the Painters). But that which had existed before him was the work of decadence and was tainted by the most severe Byzantinism It was Cimabue who infused a new spirit into the old schools in which he had studied, who renewed in man forgotten types and who first gave to inanimate forms a new life. He imbued his subjects with energy of expression, greater subtleness of outline and more delicate colouring. It was this severance from the traditions of the past which caused his efforts to be of such immense importance. This is why the father of the history of art, Georgio Vasari (1511–1574), in his work called "The Lives of the Most Eminent Painters, Sculptors, and Architects," begins his series of biographies of celebrated painters with Giovanni Cimabue.

To-day, when we are masters of technique and can so easily give an object the appearance of relief on a flat surface, we can scarcely appreciate the difficulties which in Cimabue's time had to be overcome.

In order to realize this progress as compared with past traditions, one must study Cimabue's picture, "The Virgin and Child" (No. 1260), which is to be found in

1260.   *The Virgin and Child.* — *Cimabue.*

the Salle des Primitifs in the Louvre. The Virgin appears against a background of uniform gold, severe and majestic, seated on a massive throne with the Child upon her knees. It is the gentle inclination of the head and the melancholy resignation with which the artist has softened the expression of the face which announce this new era. The Child is no longer the traditional, rigid doll. He has become animated, and a wistful expression plays over the faces of the angels, thus giving an appearance of life to a work of art for the first time. The grouping still seems primitive, the angels stand stiffly on either side of the throne, but the problem of grouping, here considered for the first time, is of capital importance. Cimabue also felt the power of colour and tried to give it greater emphasis; and, although the blue garment of the Virgin is still traditional, it is treated with a certain gracefulness of outline, and there is originality in the red band which, running round it, forms a hem, while the wings and robes of the angels are variously and richly shaded. It is especially in the colouring, however, that one clearly recognizes the still active influences of tradition and of mosaic work, for here we see no shade of gradation. The tones are placed in violent contrast to each other; what should be red in the faces is brown, and the robes of the angels are bluish pink with no intermediary shades. This great initiator only timidly attempted to interpret nature, as if he feared that the problem was beyond his powers; and so the head of the Virgin is too large, the fingers are too tapering, the chin and mouth too small and the eyes too almond-shaped.

The awakening of art from its sleep of centuries being an accomplished fact, Cimabue left the continuation of the work to his great and capable pupil, Giotto di Bondone (1276-1337).

While still living, Giotto saw his fame proclaimed by no less a poet than his friend Dante. "Cimabue believed that, in painting, he was master of the field, but, to-day, Giotto has the acclamation of the public and Cimabue's fame is overshadowed" (Purgatorio, XI-32). Cimabue was said to have found Giotto as a shepherd in a field making drawings of sheep, and was so surprised by their excellence that he took him as his pupil. Another story was that Giotto, apprenticed to a wool merchant, had so neglected his work in order to be near Cimabue that he was dismissed by his master. A little later, however, he was enabled to devote the rest of his life to the art of painting which he loved so well.

The subjects which Cimabue represented were confined by tradition to scenes from the Gospels and the Old Testament. Giotto had the good fortune to find a fertile subject in the new and touching legends connected with St. Francis of Assisi. To-day, his masterpieces are to be found in Assisi and Padua. Unfortunately, the Louvre contains only one specimen of this artist's work, "St. Francis of Assisi Receiving the Stigmata" (No. 1312), which, as well as nearly all of the pictures coming immediately under consideration, is to be found in the Salle des Primitifs. Though a valuable example of Giotto's work, this picture, unfortunately, is not entirely free from restoration. The saint is kneeling in ecstasy, stretching out his arms and raising his eyes to the figure of Christ

Musée du Louvre — St François d'Assise recevant les Stigmates, par Giotto. — Ed. H. phot.

1312. St. Francis receiving the Stigmata. — *Giotto.*   [7]

which floats above in the act of transmitting the stigmata
to the body of St. Francis. The remarkable feature of
the composition is that St. Francis' attitude of wonder
and reverence is such that the transmission of the stigmata
seems natural and suggests no physical distortion. The expression on the countenance of St. Francis is no less
remarkable; for in it we read timidity, reverence, and
astonishment, inspired by the grace imparted to him.
Up to the time of Cimabue it was the custom of artists
to wet the drapery on their models in order to make
it c'eave more closely to the body, but the robe here
is no longer treated in this primitive manner, as if glued
to the figure in parallel lines, and the amply draped garments adapt themselves to the movements of the body.
Giotto, however, confined himself to an excessive simplicity of detail in the treatment of landscape, to which
he was limited by the ignorance of perspective, characteristic of the period. The stiff trees seem pasted to the
mountain, and these, together with the buildings, bear
no relation to the figures.

Below the main picture are three small scenes relating
to the legend of St. Francis. One of them represents
the dream of Pope Innocent III to whom St. Francis
appears propping up the crumbling basilica of St. John
of Lateran. The architecture is simply suggested by
means of thin columns without proportion. The second
scene represents the Pope conferring the rules of the
Order of the Franciscans; and the third refers to the
most charming of legends — St. Francis preaching to
the birds. Here Giotto seems to have expressed something of his gentle nature, for there is a distinct dain-

tiness in each of the birds and something touching in the solicitous attitude with which St Francis so sweetly manifests his immense love for the things of nature. The paintings by Giotto connected with the legend of St. Francis of Assisi have become classic in Italian art and, more than a hundred years later, we find the same subject treated in the works of Pesellino.

The sudden progress achieved by Giotto, as compared with what had gone before, was too great to be continued by his immediate successors. The " Funeral of St. Bernard" (No. 1313), School of Giotto, shows some tendency to imitate the master's manner, but without complete success Emotion is expressed in a conventional manner; mourning, for instance, is suggested by the bowed head and raised hands; but, on the other hand, the treatment of grouping is varied and in accordance with the manner of Giotto. Some figures are in profile, while others are in full face, and the composition is clear and intelligible.

While Giotto portrayed emotion by the actual expression of the face, primitive art and Giotto's immediate successors could do so only by means of narrative Thus, in "St Francis Receiving the Stigmata," Giotto expressed awe and veneration on the countenance of the saint, whereas, in the "Funeral of St. Bernard," by a pupil, we see sorrow expressed only by means of bowed heads and raised hands. In other words, Giotto gives us the emotion itself, the others an attribute of emotion. Thus, primitive art delighted in narrative expressed by means of accessory compositions, and described in them incidents which occurred before or after the principal

event. This may be seen in "The Banquet of Herod," by
Taddeo Gaddi (1300–1366?), one shutter of a predella in
three parts consisting of the "Banquet of Herod," "The
Crucifixion," and "The Martyrdom of a Saint" (No.
1302). Here we see a warrior bringing the bleeding
head of St. John to Herod during the feast while, on the
left, in an open tower, lies the decapitated body of the
saint, and, on the right, Salome with Herodias.   In

Braun, Clement & Cie., Phot.   Salle VII

1302.   The banquet of Herod. — Part of a Predella by Taddeo Gaddi.

"The Crucifixion" of the same predella as well as in
the side panel representing "The Martyrdom of a Saint,"
we see the qualities which Giotto had taught the Floren-
tines to search for, namely, animation of movement and
expression on the countenances. In "The Crucifixion"
are to be found other new elements — the repose of the
body of the dead Saviour, and the characteristic contrast between the good and bad thief. Although, in this
picture, the colour and touch are less delicate than those
of Giotto, his influence is still very perceptible.

As the subjects treated became more complicated, technique was necessarily more and more developed; and, with technique, came the decorative element. This commenced with Taddeo (1300–1366?) and continued with Agnolo Gaddi (1343–1396). "The Annunciation" (No. 1301), by Agnolo, shows great freshness of colouring, but a lack of observation in his treatment of nature. The Virgin

E. Hautecœur, Phot.   Salle VII

1301.   The Annunciation. — Agnolo Gaddi.

is neither standing nor seated; the action of the other figures is stereotyped, and the expression of the faces is affected. We see this tendency to affectation and mannerism in "The Virgin and Child" (No. 1316), evidently a work by Agnolo Gaddi, though ascribed on the frame of the picture to the school of Giotto. Here his angels' faces are without character and all are alike; the hair is too artificially arranged, and the whole is on a uniform back-

ground of gold. In this picture the purely decorative
element overshadows the subject

We have now considered three generations of artists.
The first, with Cimabue, emancipated itself from many
Byzantine traditions. The second, with Giotto, represented emotion in the expression of the faces, mobility
and artistic grouping. In the third, with which we have
just dealt, that of Taddeo and Agnolo Gaddi, decoration
and adornment replace real feeling. In this third generation of artists, although the old Byzantine manner
seems to have disappeared, this is not entirely the case,
for, as often happens when one form of art ceases to
exist and a new form is not perfected, a return to the point
of departure took place, and, with this return, appeared
former archaic elements. Thus we see in "The Virgin
and Child" (No 1315), by a pupil of Giotto, the narrow
eyes, the conventional pose and the garment covering
the feet; in a word, all the elements with which Cimabue
had had to contend.

While religious subjects continued to conform to tradition, secular scenes began to change into representations
of the actual life of the period. Even "The Birth of St.
John the Baptist" (No. 1317), by a pupil of Giotto, with
all its awkwardness, is a little scene representing the life
and conditions of the fourteenth century. Two women
stand near St Elizabeth ministering to her, while an aged
woman bends over and plays with the new-born Child
and presents Him with a flower. It was with such works
as these, in spite of all their shortcomings, that art was
born again; and the three subsequent centuries owe the
origin of their wonderful creations to these beginnings.

At the commencement of the fifteenth century Italy was in a condition of continuous internal political strife. Divided into innumerable little states all fighting each other with implacable hatred, the clearest political foresight could not predict the possibility of a national unity. It was only that extraordinary man, Cæsar Borgia, who first dreamed of this. But these conditions of isolation and these political struggles for supremacy were peculiarly advantageous to art; and, side by side with the art of Florence, grew up innumerable local schools of a lower order in many respects and without any character of their own Each, according to its own individuality, contributed to form the art of the *Renaissance*, and, after an existence more or less long, they were finally absorbed by the great master schools

The natural counterpart of the art of Florence is that of the school of Siena. This city, in political rivalry with its powerful neighbour, also had an ambition to struggle with Florence in the domain of art. What Cimabue had done for Florence, Duccio did for Siena. It is greatly to be regretted that there is no picture by Duccio in the Louvre.

On the 19th of June, 1310, a solemn procession went to Duccio's house to fetch the picture of "The Virgin Enthroned," destined for the high altar of the cathedral, and carried it there to the sound of bells, drums, and trumpets; and there it may still be seen in its original position This date marks the official recognition of Siena as the rival of Florence in painting.

The essential and fundamental difference between the two Schools consisted in this, that, while Cimabue transformed Byzantine art, Duccio perfected it even though he retained its manner. Notwithstanding the considerable progress realised by Duccio's successors, the Memmis and the Lorenzettis, the Sienese school was destined to perish because its art erred from its very starting point.

"The Virgin and Child, The Nativity and The Crucifixion" (No. 1667), a tryptich by an unknown master, presents all the characteristics of the primitive manner of Siena. The pose of the Virgin is rigid, and her type vividly recalls the Byzantine models, but there is an improvement. The Child, whom she holds upon her knees, turns with an easy motion toward the angels who adore Him and, at the foot of the throne, are some figures playing on musical instruments. The grouping of these figures is in uniform lines, the composition is simple and natural, the action is dignified and measured, and the types, though still primitive, are full of expression. We find the same characteristics in the representation of tragic subjects, as in "The Crucifixion" (No. 1665) by an unknown master. Here an attempt at symmetry in the grouping may be distinctly seen in the horsemen at the sides of the picture.

Siena clung to Byzantine traditions in interpreting sacred subjects and became the model for the treatment of sacred art in all Italy. To this day we still see a **survival** of the Byzantine manner in the handling of certain religious subjects. We find in Siena the most charming works of this kind, such as those of Simone Memmi (1283–1344), to whom, as the worthy rival of Zeuxis, Petrarch dedicated some eulogistic sonnets (Nos. 57 and 58). It is in his types of the Virgin that Memmi shows his greatest power.

An example of this is "The Virgin Enthroned" which may be seen in the public palace at Siena, and in which

E. Hautecœur, Phot.   Salle VII

1383.   The March to Calvary. — Memmi.

there remains none of the green flesh-tint peculiar to the Byzantine school.

Simone Memmi painted in clear and distinct tones.

The movements are calm, the grouping symmetrical, and the expression of emotion is natural. His manner was so individual and so firmly ingrained that even his stay at Assisi and Avignon as successor to Giotto made no change in it. This is plainly to be seen in "The March to Calvary" (No. 1383). We admire the fine, miniature-like execution, the vigor and purity of the tones and the expression on the face of St. Mary Magdalene. But arrangement and composition were not within the power of Siena at this period. The figures form a motley mass; they are simply placed one beside the other, and the detail, though rich, is almost overloaded. Simone Memmi succeeds in making the figure of Christ the centre of the composition by representing Him walking while the others stand still. By this apparently simple artifice, the figure of Christ occupies more space, and it is also striking by reason of the bright red tone of His garments.

Umbria, Ferrara, and Bologna almost entirely adopted the manner of Siena, namely, fidelity to Byzantine traditions. The same applies to Pisa, and the work of Turino Vanni (end of 14th century), in his "Virgin and Child" (No. 1563), may be taken as an example of the art of that city at this period.

With the Lorenzetti brothers, of whose work there is no example in the Louvre, the painting of Siena attained its highest point. To the vigorous drawing of Giotto and the flexible action of Pisano they added depth of sentiment. Their pupils and successors had, perhaps, their skill, but not their greatness. We see this in Bartolo di Maestro Fredi's (1330–1410) "Presentation in the Temple" (No. 1151), which, notwithstanding the delicate execution,

Salle VII

1151.   *The Presentation in the Temple.* — *Fredi.*

especially of the hair, the flexibility and arrangement
of the garments, the natural attitude of the Infant Jesus,
is lacking in all individual character.

But the original creative power of Siena was soon exhausted, and there was a return to the primitive manner. In "St. Peter" (No. 1152), by Taddeo di Bartolo (1363–1422), we see a voluntary return to the old archaism. St. Peter's proportions are short and heavy, there is no vividness in the colouring and a monotonous yellow tint predominates. The full face figure has no action.

Sano di Pietro (1405–1481), wrongly called the Fra

E. Hautecœur, Phot.   Salle VII

1128. The Dream of St. Jerome. — Sano di Pietro.

Angelico of Siena, is the last of the Epigones, or weak followers of great predecessors. His greatest quality was his indefatigable diligence, though even this has been questioned. One cannot find in him any of the ingenuous qualities of Fra Angelico. We do not admire his cycle of "The Legend of St. Jerome" (Nos. 1128–1132) where the proportions are bad, and the figures are not well grouped. The perspective of the architecture in No. 1128, the first picture of this series, is treated with a certain mastery and forms a contrast with the stiff simplcity of the trees in No 1130 which seem borrowed from a box of toys An original feature of Sano di Pietro's pictures was their grey fields, brown trees and mountains crowned with red castles.

It was not until the end of the sixteenth century that a new life was given to the art of Siena by Sodoma and Peruzzi

The Florentine school and the followers of the Gaddis would have fallen into similar mannerisms if, shortly before the appearance of Masaccio, of whose work there is unfortunately no example in the Louvre, the old art had not said its last word in the charming and harmonious works of Fra Angelico.

Angelico was preceded by Don Lorenzo Monaco (1370–1425) whose " Picture in Three Parts" (No 1348), containing figures of St Lawrence, St Agnes, and St. Marguerite, was, even at that early period, a piece of beautiful, clear and bright colouring. Its treatment, though not entirely free, is, perhaps for that very reason, not less warm and charming. In " The Prayer in the Garden of Olives" (No 1348A), by the same artist, a picture in two parts, the figure of Christ with the sleeping disciples is placed below in the narrow space of a half shutter, and this already shows a power of concentration and grouping which announces the coming of a new era.

As to the old school, it comes to an end with one of the most charming of its interpreters, namely Fra Angelico

FRA ANGELICO TO ANTONELLO DA MESSINA.

A LTHOUGH to us Fra Giovanni da Fiesole, called il
Angelico (1387–1455), seems to represent the end of a
long period in the history of art, he is, nevertheless, the
great creator of a new epoch in his power of giving expression to sentiment with greater delicacy and truth than
his predecessors. Vasari says of him· "This truly angelic
brother consecrated his life to the service of God and
of his neighbour and held himself aloof from all things
worldly. He painted all his life, but was never willing to
paint anything but sacred subjects. 'He who,' Fra Angelico says, 'wishes to represent the works of Christ should
always live in the society of Christ.' What he painted
he did not retouch nor correct, for he thought that God
wished it to remain as it was. It is said that he never
took the brush in his hand without previous prayer, and
that he never painted the Crucifixion without tears rolling
down his face; and this is why we see the strength and
sincerity of his faith in the features and attitudes of his
persons. There is something of his soul in everything
that he did, and he only worked when under the influence
of divine love."

It is very difficult to fix upon the exact period in which
a new idea is born. Thus, we cannot assign a precise
date to the disappearance of the gold background, though
this is of no great importance. Fra Angelico, by discard-
ing this artificial adornment, gave to his pictures the appearance of air and space

E. Hautecœur, Phot. Salle VII

1290. The Coronation of the Virgin. — Fra Angelico.

This we see in "The Coronation of the Virgin" (No. 1290), where the deep blue background conveys the illusion of the sky. This work is mentioned by Vasari as one of Fra Angelico's masterpieces. Fra Angelico represented the scene as taking place in heaven, and the increasingly darker shades of blue seem to indicate other ethereal spaces in the distance This effect Fra Angelico created without effort. The tone of the picture is light and brilliant, and blue, red, and gold shades predominate. On a high throne Christ is seated majestically, though without severity, and His inclination toward the Virgin is full of gentleness and filial love. The Virgin seems inspired with maternal tenderness, her arms are crossed upon her bosom and she affectionately turns toward her Son in an attitude of humility A large assembly of angels and saints surrounds the throne; some are enraptured, others bow humbly, and all are deeply interested in the scene. The strings vibrate, the viols resound, and the trumpets are turned to all parts of the heavens in praise of the Lord and to celebrate the crowning of the Mother of God. The trumpets in the background also give us a sensation of vast distance filled with graceful figures, and a flood of happiness emanates from this inspired composition

We experience the same sensation when we study the predella, or accessory scenes, below the main picture, representing Christ rising from the dead and the legend of St. Francis executed in miniature. Even when Fra Angelico painted tragic scenes, as "The Martyrdom of St. Cosmo and St. Damian" (No 1293), he treated the subject humanely. For, though the saint's head is separated from the trunk and drips with blood, the artist spares us details connected with the executioner by making him turn his back upon us. He also makes the picture less painful by placing the scene in a charming landscape. When he was not treating scenes laid in heaven, he simply imitated the manner of Giotto, as in "The Beheading of St. John the Baptist" (No. 1291). Interior subjects and tragic scenes were not congenial to him since they did not allow of any landscape. His

E. Hautecœur. Phot.   Salle VII

1291. The Beheading of St. John the Baptist. — Fra Angelico.

domain was the clear and radiant sky. This, again, we see in "The Resurrection" (No. 1294 A) where the Redeemer is represented in all His majesty, robed in an ample white garment, with eyes raised to heaven.

It is not absolute truth which we find in the work of Fra Angelico, but relative truth. It is the perfect harmony of his sentiments, together with his manner of treating subjects sympathetic to him, which constitutes the real value of his work. This is why Fra Angelico's work conveys a simple and natural impression. His composi-

E. Hautecœur, Phot.   Salle VII

1307. The Virgin and Child. — Neri di Bicci.

tion is not artificial and the effect is artistic, for he had the temperament of a true artist.

All the other artists of the school of Gaddi, in comparison with Fra Angelico, seem simple artisans. Neri di Bicci (1419–1491), is an example of this, as may be seen in his "Virgin and Child" (No. 1397)

The art of Florence was at a deadlock, and an original genius was necessary to avert the danger of a return to archaism such as took place at Siena Such a genius was Masaccio (1401–1429) He represented an evolution in the power of giving expression which was to serve not Florentine art alone, but all schools and all times He was a pupil of Masolino, he studied perspective with Brunelleschi, art with Donatello, and mathematics with Manetti His strong individuality was able to assimilate all these branches of knowledge, and he was an accomplished master at the age of twenty Unhappily his career was cut short at the age of twenty-eight, and he died, ruined by debts and in misery, in 1429. His best works are in the Brancacci Chapel at Florence.

Unfortunately there are none of Masaccio's works in the Louvre, but the most characteristic picture of his school is "The Entrance of Pope Martin V into the Castle of St Angelo" (No 1659 A). The qualities which characterise the manner of Masaccio are only vaguely indicated here and do not adequately show the progress attained. The qualities peculiarly his were strength, natural beauty of form, realism in the action of the figures, sincerity of expression, dignity of gesture, flexible amplitude and richness in the treatment of drapery To these must be added a very important element, the treatment of shadows, which alone makes the representation of relief on a flat surface possible This enabled him to introduce perspective into his landscapes and, thus, to deal with the question of horizon. These are the conquests which Masaccio has bequeathed to posterity.

The times in which Masaccio lived were full of action, innovation and contradictory aspirations. By the side of the gentle art of Fra Angelico and of the classical realism of Masaccio, we find the simple observation of nature which characterises Paolo Uccello (1397–1475). He began by being a sculptor and only made use of

E. Hautecœur, Phot.   Salle VII

1273.   A Battle. — Paolo Uccello.

painting in order to study the problems of perspective and make other experiments. This fact we see illustrated in his picture "A Battle" (No. 1273), for the figures stand out from the surroundings, without any distribution of light, like silhouettes on a black background. The faces show no trace of life, for the problem of expression did not interest him. On the other hand, his power of observation is remarkable, as may be seen in his treatment of the horses. The palfreys in the foreground rear and turn their heads violently to one side, and this constitutes a picturesque problem in perspective. The same applies to the horses in the background on the right, with their varied positions and the confusion of their limbs. All this is produced without any concern for beauty which is outraged by the long, straight lances which traverse the picture. Thus, in the first half of the fifteenth century, we find ourselves in the presence of a brutal realism born of a deep and irresistible desire for truth and a too careful observation of detail.

Problems such as these alone interested Paolo Uccello. The picture (No. 1272) in which he represented himself in company with Giotto, Brunelleschi, Donatello, and Manetti shows his weak points rather than his good qualities. The features are hard, and Uccello does not seek to represent character, but rather, if we may say so, to give us a photograph.[1]

While Uccello was thus trying to solve certain problems, and while Fra Angelico was producing his works full of charm and devotion in the silence of the cloister, another monk of a very different temperament was developing art from the point where Masaccio had left it This was Fra Filippo Lippi (1406?-1469), a characteristic type of his period. Unlike Fra Angelico, he did not paint for the glory of God, but because he loved art and nature for their own sakes. He was an orphan at an early age and, as an inmate of the Convent of the Carmelites, probably assisted Masaccio in the decoration of the Brancacci Chapel. From this monastery he fled and, after many changes of fortune, married the nun, Lucretia Buti But, notwithstanding his irregularities, he was powerfully protected because of his talent.

In religious subjects, as, for instance, in his "Virgin and Infant Jesus" (No. 1344), he confined himself to the treatment of the foreground in order to avoid the problem of perspective. The Virgin is no longer celestial, as with Fra

Braun, Clement & Cie., Phot.   Salle VII

1344.   The Virgin and Infant Jesus. — Lippi.

Angelico, but of this earth, notwithstanding her ideal expression and the graceful oval of her face. Her pose is easy, with one knee slightly turned to the side—a position which Filippo Lippi particularly affected, and which may be noticed in the angel on the left. Among modern painters, Burne-Jones has borrowed this detail. The Virgin holds the Child lightly pressed against her, yet

the element of weight seems disregarded and He appears
to float. This artifice is also used by Michael Angelo
in his treatment of the tomb of the Medicis. The two
monks in Lippi's picture have very distinct characteristics. The one, with a grave and stern expression, shows
himself to be an ascetic; while the other, with his gentle
look, is of a softer nature. On all sides are grouped
angels with no particular expression of piety, round-
faced children of this earth, some of them not even taking
any interest in the scene. But peace reigns throughout
the composition, the shading is well done, the drapery
falls gracefully, and the whole makes us understand the
admiration which, according to Vasari, Lippi's contemporaries felt for his work

With Filippo Lippi begins that familiar representation
of the Holy Family from which religious and mystic elements disappear, and something purely human takes their
place. The art of Raphael is, as we know, the most perfect expression of this new spirit

We see this human element again in "The Nativity"
(No 1343), mentioned by Vasari and attributed to
Pesellino by Crowe and Cavalcaselle.[2] Here is a wide
and charming landscape enlivened by a river A town
and lake appear in a background which is studded with
wooded hills and intersected by valleys which allow glimp-
ses into the distance In the foreground in the midst of
the ruins of a house is a thatched hut and a stable containing an ox and an ass Before these the Virgin is
leaning over the Child in an attitude of love and
adoration, while St. Joseph, to the right, observes
Him with a stern look of amazement. The Child lies

in the centre of the picture between the Virgin and St.
Joseph and a curious detail may be noticed in the fact

E. Hautecœur, Phot.   Salle VII

1343.   The Nativity. — Lippi.

that the edges of their garments, passing under the body
of the Infant, form the couch on which He lies. The simplicity of the landscape and general details of the picture
accentuate the importance of the principal scene, as com-

pared with the rest of the composition. A shepherd, in the middle distance, plays the flute in the midst of his flock, and three others, in a far part of the landscape, are engaged in animated conversation. The Child is not a Divine Being, but a human child. His cheeks are rosy, and he has His little fingers in His mouth like all other babies. The Virgin also is entirely of this world, notwithstanding the presence of the two angels giving their blessing from above and of the dove representing the Holy Ghost. As befits a scene in the open air, the tones of the picture are light and clear, giving the whole composition a graceful and cheerful appearance, in spite of the many elements which figure in it. This is not a picture representing mysticism, but only earthly joy and happiness.

The influence of **Fra Filippo Lippi** on his contemporaries was immense. He was essentially worldly, and, in his time, worldliness permeated the higher clergy no less than the rest of the community. The unknown painter of "The Virgin and Infant Jesus" (No. 1661 A), in the same room, imitates him, without any personal characteristic. He has borrowed from Fra Filippo Lippi the full arch which frames the Virgin, the soft oval of her face, the graceful manner in which she supports the feet of the Child and also the way in which the blues and reds are placed side by side. But the colour and drawing are weaker and less individual than with Lippi.

Among the best disciples of this school was Stefano Pesellino (1422–1457), and the influence of Lippi on his work was remarkably blended with archaic elements. "The Stigmatisation of St. Francis" (No. 1414), a picture in two parts, seem to be borrowed from Giotto. Pesellino died young, and during his short life his energies were always directed to technical problems connected with paints and their solvents, subjects which, before the introduction of painting in oils, a tracted much attention in Italy. Traces of his experiments are to be seen

Braun, Clement & Cie., Phot.   Salle VII

1414. The Stigmatisation of St. Francis. — Pesellino.

in his colouring which is always heavy and dark. The same characteristics are found in the second panel of the same picture, "St. Cosmo and St. Damian Ministering to a sick Person." Little that is worthy of Pesellino is to be seen in his other work, "The Dead Christ" (No. 1415), a picture in three parts.

We have now arrived at the point where the deep religious feeling of Fra Angelico and the worldly characteristics of Filippo Lippi were blended. This fusion took place in the school of Benozzo Gozzoli (1424–after 1496). Influenced by the pious Fra Angelico, he withdrew from the world and retired to the solitude of Montefeltre. "The Virgin Surrounded by Saints" (No. 1320), with predella and side pictures, is not by him, but was inspired by him.

The influence of Fra Angelico is visible in the faces of the
Virgin and Child, in the treatment of the light blue
garment with yellow borders and in the sweetness and
softness of the faces in the background, as well as in the
large halos and gilded ornaments. St. Thomas, on the
right side of the picture, wears an expression of gentleness characteristic of Fra Angelico's manner, but the three
other saints in the foreground, St Francis, St John, and
particularly St. Jerome, have an energy of expression more
after the manner of Fra Filippo Lippi This is an excellent
example of the fusion of the schools of Fra Angelico and
Fra Filippo Lippi The landscape and the rich foliage
of the bushes in the background afterwards inspired
Lippi's industrious pupil, Sandro Botticelli. The little
pictures which surround the composition again reveal,
by the dominating light blue colouring, the influence of
Fra Angelico A lingering love for the archaic caused
the artist to introduce this element into the picture thereby reminding us of Fra Angelico's " Martyrdom of St Cosmo and St Damian " (No. 1293) and of his " Resurrection"
(No. 1294 A) both of which we have already considered.[3]

Benozzo Gozzoli was not a seeker nor an innovator
and only blended the characteristics he found existing and
made them harmonious. "The Triumph of St. Thomas
Aquinas" (No. 1319), considered his best picture, is the
one which, perhaps, least shows his characteristics, for he
imitated a peculiar composition created by Traini St.
Thomas is enthroned between Plato and Aristotle, with
his adversary vanqu shed at his feet, while, in the lower
part of the picture, we see the assembled clergy pro-
claiming the glory of the saint. The face, as a por-

trait, is treated in a masterly manner. The eyelids are heavy, and the thoughtful brow is lined with wrinkles.

E. Hautecœur, Phot.   Salle VII

*1319.   The Triumph of St. Thomas
Aquinas. — Gozzoli.*

The natural expressions of the Fathers of the Church are also remarkable, although the similarity of their positions and the manner of grouping so many persons in so small a space show that the knowledge of concentration had not yet been mastered.

Lessing, the great German seeker after truth, has written: "If God were to address me, saying, 'In the one hand I hold the Search for Truth, in the other Truth itself. Choose between the two' — I would bow down and say, 'Lord, to Thee alone belongs Truth. We can only seek it.'" It is, perhaps, this very sentiment which makes us so appreciative of the immense efforts which the fifteenth century made to reproduce nature and to express human emotion. The curtain rose slowly, but we

see that every artist assimilated any innovation made by his
predecessor and, in his turn, improved upon it, for art like
nature does not develop in leaps and bounds, but gradually.

E. Hautecœur, Phot.   Salle VII

1300 B.   The Virgin and Child. — Piero di Francesca.

It is only in little details that we are able to trace the
strenuous efforts made by some of these men, as, for instance, in the case of Alessio Baldovinetti (1427–1499),
whose somewhat unsuccessful technical experiments
doomed his work to early oblivion. As far as we can

judge of him by what remains of his work, he was a cold and determined realist, with great power of observation; rather a seeker after art than a true artist It is this which inclines us to attribute to him a picture, "The Virgin and Child" (No. 1300 B) which bears the signature of Piero della Francesca (1423–1492). The Virgin gently bends forward and contemplates the Divine Child. The colour of the face of the Virgin is cold and clear, as is the scheme of the whole picture, recalling the even tones of the pictures of the past A scarcely perceptible smile plays on her features. The Child is much too small to be in harmony with the *ensemble* and has, furthermore, the serious and intelligent look of an adult. There is nothing here of the penetration and charm of Filippo Lippi, for the problems studied by Baldovinetti were only those of colour and perspective Thus, the red cushion constitutes the striking feature of the picture, and the gauze which covers it shows delicacy of treatment. The vanishing point is placed far enough away for us to discern a vast extent of landscape. The vegetation is too minutely realistic, and the trees are placed too far in the background, but the atmosphere is very transparent, giving lightness and freedom to the composition.

Verrocchio (1435–1488) was destined to furnish the last element necessary to the development of fifteenth century art. Though, at first, only a sculptor, his knowledge of the Arts and Sciences, as they then existed, seems to have been complete This knowledge he imparted to Lionardo da Vinci, to Perugino and Lorenzo di Credi. That his hand was accustomed to hard metal and the chisel is shown by his energy in the handling

E. Hautecœur, Phot.   Salle VII

1482.   The Virgin in Glory. — Verrocchio.

of the brush, and his theoretical researches and the
conscientiousness with which he studied his subject gave
to his drawing the clearness of carving.   As Vasari says:
"One sees that his precision, which borders on hardness,
is the result of indefatigable study rather than of observation of nature, or the outcome of a natural gift."   A

man of Verrochio's acquirements was born to be at the
head of a school.

As a sculptor, he was the greatest of the successors of
Donatello, but, as a painter, his works were too hard, a
defect which appears, for instance, in his treatment of
horses, which have a look of being flayed.

"The Virgin in Glory" (No. 1482), which we must
attribute to Verrocchio, presents all the characteristics
of his works. This picture was formerly attributed to Roselli di Lorenzo Filippo (1439–1507) and, by some critics,
to Cosimo. In a blue sky, the Virgin, seated on a throne,
is surrounded by rays of light in the midst of which float
the heads of angels. She offers a piece of fruit to the
Child, whose expression is severe and earnest. He stands
upon her knee and turns toward St. Anthony who contemplates Him with devotion, while St. Mary the Egyptian kneels in humble ecstasy. On the sides, angels,
whose garments and attitudes indicate rapid flight, seem
to stop suddenly before the Virgin. This remarkable
work is a many-sided problem. The robes of the saints
have the distinctness of enamel, with heavy shadows in
the folds; the hair of Mary the Egyptian is as if carved
in bronze, and the heads of the angels are like fine pieces
of jewelry. All this bears witness to the influence which
the sculptor element in Verrocchio had on his painting.
The severe beauty of the Virgin's face, and the variety of
expression on the faces of the angels have another origin;
for they have something of the manner of Botticelli,
while the Infant Jesus irresistibly recalls the simple
grandeur of Boltraffio. The brilliancy of the colours is
due to their juxtaposition rather than to their own values.

E. Hautecœur, Phot.   Salle VII

1263.   The Virgin and Child. — Lorenzo di Credi.

The influence of Verrocchio is only slightly seen in a picture of his school, otherwise of little merit, "Esther before Ahasuerus" (No. 1643 A) and consists in the careful modelling of the garments of the persons in movement.[4] As Verrocchio produced little himself, we can best judge of him from the work of one of the most important of his numerous pupils, Lorenzo di Credi (1459–1537) who has most faithfully preserved his manner.

The Louvre possesses in "The Virgin and Child with St. Julian and St Nicholas" (No. 1263), a work in which, according to Vasari, Lorenzo di Credi surpassed himself. The details are of a painful minuteness and seem to have the polish of ivory; the drawing is rigorously correct, but the modelling of the faces, especially that of St. Nicholas, is of a metallic hardness. There is here a singular blending of different influences, as if the manner of the various pupils of Verrocchio were united in one man. The face of the Virgin wears the sweet expression peculiar to Perugino, and St. Julian, by his contemplative look and by the inclination of the body, recalls the great Francia of Bologna Lorenzo di Credi was not a marked innovator, otherwise he would not have allowed St. Julian and St. Nicholas to shut out the landscape, neither would he have permitted the grey and monotonous wall to withdraw attention from the Virgin who is the principal figure of the composition.

It is easy to exaggerate the importance of such a picture and the talent of the artist. His "Noli me tangere" (No. 1264) enables us to form a more correct judgment. Here, again, are the polish, the precision and careful execution of enamel, but breadth of drawing and concentration of the different elements are lacking; for, though the landscape has charm and brightness, the scattering of the subjects seems to make of the picture two different compositions.

In the fifteenth century each decade seemed to bring forth a great man, but there is one who is particularly associated with the latter part of that century, Sandro Botticelli (1446–1510). He put into his pictures a spiritual element unknown and unsuspected before. He has not the brilliant manner of Ghirlandajo, nor the worldly language of Filippo Lippi, but a treatment all his own, full

E. Hautecœur, Phot.   Salle VII

1295. *The Virgin writing the Magnificat.* — *Botticelli.*

of mysticism and beauty drawn from his very soul. In his pictures, slender figures of maidens appear in all their severe grace, with mysterious, earnest expressions, while fields of fantasy and fairy-like splendour are drawn from the strange world of dreams.

Little is known of Botticelli's life. He was born in Florence and was already famous when his master, Fra Filippo Lippi, died in 1469. He was called by Pope Sixtus IV (1470–1484) to decorate the Sistine Chapel in Rome. At a certain period of his life, a great change took place in the nature of Botticelli, but it is difficult to state the precise moment. It may have been during his stay in Rome, but it is more likely that it was due to the influence of Savonarola after his return to Florence. The fierce indignation preached by this monk against the world seems to have had an influence on all Botticelli's later creations. His Virgins, formerly dreamy and mystical, became forbidding, almost stern. Botticelli has been only recently appreciated, but modern criticism has placed him in the front rank of great artists and has taught us the value of his work. "The Virgin Writing the Magnificat" (No. 1295) is a contemporary copy of the original in Florence and is one of his finest productions. One angel offers her a book and ink into which she dips a pen, while another holds a crown above her head. Her eyes are sad and serious, as if she foresaw all the suffering to come; and the Child upon her knees touches her arm lightly and raises His eyes with a look of sympathy and comprehension. The hair of the Virgin and angels reminds us of the jeweller's art which Botticelli first learned His ideal of beauty, in this and other works, seems to consist in a long, oval face with clear-cut chin somewhat square at the extremity. The circular shape of this picture, as well as the close grouping of the figures is remarkable. The picture is not cramped, for the landscape suggests space and gives it an impression of ease and freedom.

1296.   The Virgin, the Infant Jesus and St. John. — Botticelli.

Another work by Botticelli, "The Virgin, the Infant Jesus and St. John" (No. 1296), is full of the same note of sadness. The graceful motion with which the

Virgin encircles the Child standing on her knee and the
look of pity she casts on Him, reveal the intensity of her
love. The Child gently caresses His Mother as if He
wished to comfort her for the calamities which are to
come, and as if He desired to make her know that His
suffering was to be for the salvation of the world. This
work is drawn from the very soul of the artist, and the
wistful look with which St. John observes us seems to
ask if we too are not touched. This little figure is, perhaps, the most beautiful in the composition. Here, also,
are a clear blue sky and delicate flowering bushes, em-
blems of hope.

Other works of Botticelli show clearly how much his
talent was in danger of suffering from an exaggerated
sentimentality. His power in the representation of movement and floating drapery is seen in the frescoes from
the Villa Lemmi (No. 1297), now on the Escalier Daru
opposite the Flying Victory of Samothrace. On the other
hand, his ability to represent individual types is very man-
ifest in the masterly "Portrait of a Man" (No. 1663)
which, though not attributed to him, can be by no one
else   Here, the severe face and compressed lips show de-
termination of character, the eyes have a steely look, and
the modelling of the cheeks is admirably clear.[5] We
see that the subject of this picture knew his own mind
and knew how to bend others to it, and, in order to give
further expression to this characteristic, the tone of the
picture is metallic and almost cold.

Mourning and mystic sadness were peculiar to Botticelli alone, for we see no trace of them in the works of
his contemporaries   For instance, in "The Virgin and

Child" (No. 1300 A) probably by an unknown master, the figures, the grouping and even the colouring are in the manner of Botticelli, but the Child is a child of this earth, and the features of the Virgin do not express yearning and sadness, but joy and repose. The angels have nothing hard nor clean-cut reminding us of the jeweller

Even prior to the influence of Savonarola, Botticelli never sufficiently felt the charms of the antique to make him paint statuesque figures When he represented Greek mythological subjects, he remained purely Florentine. "The Reposing Venus" (No. 1299), so characteristic of his manner, though surely not painted by him, is a work of his school and still remains the ideal of Florentine beauty. The colouring is pale, almost green; the picture is empty, but the type of face is distinctly that of Botticelli, the type imitated in the nineteenth century by Burne-Jones.

In Domenico Ghirlandajo (1449–1494) all the influences of the fifteenth century are united. He was a pupil of Alessandro Baldovinetti and in him are concentrated the grandeur of Masaccio, the movement of Verrocchio and the joyousness of Filippo Lippi His energies were such that he wished to decorate in fresco all the walls of the fortifications of Florence

He resembled Masaccio and Michael Angelo, in that he could find full expression only in large frescoes In "The Visitation" (No. 1321), dated 1491, the Louvre possesses one of the best of his works The composition, though apparently simple, is exceedingly studied The Virgin bends toward St. Elizabeth who is kneeling before her, while there is a young woman on either side. The problem to be solved was how to give importance to the two central stooping figures as contrasted with the

E. Hautecœur, Phot.   Salle VII

1321.　The Visitation. — D. Ghirlandajo.

two persons standing erect. Ghirlandajo obtains this result by placing the Virgin and St. Elizabeth in the open space against the landscape and the other two figures in front of a wall painted in neutral colours.

The perspective of the landscape is treated in a masterly manner. The colouring also blends harmoniously with the general composition. The minor figures in

E. Hautecœur, Phot.   Salle VII

1322. Old Man and Child. — D. Ghirlandajo.

the background are painted in light colours in order that they may stand out more distinctly. The blue of the Virgin's cloak is enhanced by the red garments. St. Elizabeth is kneeling and is robed in bright yellow, whereas, if she had been in sombre colours, she would have created a void in the scheme of colouring.

Even admitting that Ghirlandajo did not possess the depth and dreamy beauty of Botticelli, nor his love of detail in nature, one must recognise that he was his equal in the art of interpreting feeling. This we see in the "Portrait of an Old Man and Child" (No. 1322), a sym-

E. Hautecœur, Phot.   Salle VII

1367.   The Virgin and Child. — Mainardi.

phony in red. The old man, with all his ugliness, is carefully treated, and there is so much love in his eyes and such affectionate confidence in the look of the child, that we must believe the little one to be his grandson.

Domenico Ghirlandajo died, a victim to the plague, in 1494, at the age of forty-five, leaving a rich inheritance to the artistic world.

His first imitator was his brother-in-law and faithful assistant, Bastiano Mainardi (1470–1513) who, though not so famous an artist, nevertheless, put more feeling into his work. This is shown in his beautiful picture of "The Virgin and Child" (No. 1367). There is a particu-

E. Hautecœur, Phot.   Salle VII

1323. Christ on the Way to Calvary. — B. Ghirlandajo.

lar sweetness in the Virgin as she tenderly draws St. John the Baptist toward her. In the picture "The Virgin and Infant Jesus" (No. 1367 A), attributed to Mainardi, though the figure of Christ might be by him, the composition, as a whole, reminds us of the more primitive manner of Baldovinetti.

Domenico Ghirlandajo's younger brother, Benedetto (1458–1497), was certainly not the equal of Mainardi.

Benedetto's "Christ on the Way to Calvary" (No. 1323) is confused and cold in composition, too bright in colouring and too minutely detailed. The morbid search for expression almost distorts the face. Too great precision of this kind, though it may show conscientious work, does not take the place of talent, for, although this precision in a man of genius is easy to understand, in an imitator, it becomes affected and unreal. This is clearly seen in the unpleasing picture in question where the perspective is incoherent and poorly understood, and the action is exaggerated.

Florence had thus reached a point from which it was possible for the wonderful art of the sixteenth century to be evolved.

We have seen the art of Siena perish in archaic mannerism, but Umbria escaped this pernicious influence. Here now appeared the great Piero della Francesca (1423–1492). He was the father of the Umbro-Florentine School, and, besides having the spirit of observation, was theoretically and practically master of perspective, as is shown by his book "Prospectiva Pingendi." Two other masters of this school stand out prominently, Melozzo da Forli and Luca Signorelli.

The school of Melozzo is only feebly represented in the Louvre by the work of his pupil Palmeggiani (1456–after 1537), "The Dead Christ" (No. 1400), where the Saviour is represented in a half recumbent position, supported by angels. The yellow colour, the unsuccessful attempt to display the stigmata and the lack of expression on the faces of the angels make this artist seem essentially provincial, and he owes his reputation to his

collaboration with his great master. When Melozzo died
in 1494, Palmeggiani dropped back into his former medi-
ocrity.

Luca Signorelli (1441–1523), a pupil of Piero della
Francesca, was the most illustrious of the Umbro-Florentine school. In the works of his maturity, by his mastery
of perspective, his treatment of the nude and the manner
of his grouping, he was the real precursor of Michael
Angelo. His love of large subjects adapted itself better
to mural decoration than to painting on canvas. The

Braun, Clement & Cie., Phot.   Salle VII

1525.   The Birth of the Virgin. — Signorelli.

work which best characterises him is his predella, "The
Birth of the Virgin" (No. 1525). St. Anne presents the
new-born child to one of her attendants, and St. Joachim,
on one side, is seated writing, while a man clothed in red
is bending over the foot of the couch. The composition
is concentrated in a small space and is of remarkable
brilliancy. The young girl standing is dignified and calm.
The colour, as is almost always the case with Signorelli,
is not very strong and has grey-brown, dark shadows,
but it is employed in a manner which promises further progress. A ray of light penetrates softly through

the half open door, gently touching all the figures and thus uniting them.

In the fragment of a large composition called "Seven Persons Standing" (No. 1527), by Signorelli, we see again the brown-grey in the faces and notice that metallic distinctness which clearly bears witness to the influence of Verrocchio's work on all his contemporaries.

In the Long Gallery, on the wall opposite the entrance to the Salle des Primitifs, may be seen "The Adoration of the Magi" (No. 1526), the largest of the Italian pictures in the Louvre. It was painted by Signorelli in 1493 for San Agostino in Citta di Castello, but does not show the artist at his best. The principal feature of this picture is the Virgin with the Infant Jesus on her knees. To Him one of the kings is presenting a vase of perfume, while St. Joseph, behind the Virgin, leans upon his staff in conversation with the Moorish king. This, the most important scene, is dwarfed by the numerous horsemen in the background and by the page holding a chalice in his hands; and the colouring is cold and almost harsh owing to the juxtaposition of the crude reds. The perspective does not sufficiently produce an open-air effect, although the treatment of the fortress in the extreme background is excellent. The sides of the picture are crowded with figures, and a cramped effect is thereby produced. To the school of Signorelli belong, likewise, the fragments of a large composition (No. 1677) representing four persons standing before a portico.

Thus Signorelli and his school furnish the links between the Umbrian art, which had its origin in Siena, and the great art of Florence, and represent one of the most important features in the artistic history of all time.

E. Hautecœur, Phot. Salle VI

1526. The Adoration of the Magi. — Signorelli.

The art of the fifteenth century was not confined to large cities. Every political centre, that is to say, every independent township, possessed its peculiar and characteristic art, more or less developed. Thus, Vittore Pisano, called Pisanello (1380?–1451), was one of those original artists produced by Verona at the end of the fourteenth

century. This city was under the double influence of
Venice and Padua. Pisanello was, peculiarly, a great
medallist and gave to his pictures the quality of medals.

E. Hautecœur, Phot.   Salle VII

1422 A.   Portrait of a Princess of Este. — Pisanello.

A specimen of this work is his splendid "Portrait of a
Princess of Este" (No. 1422 A), to be found in Salle
VII.   The head, as if chiselled in bronze, stands
out from the hard foliage, and the parallel folds of
the garment as well as the embroidery on the cloak

seem to be carved rather than painted. The picture
is evidently an excellent portrait; the flowers and butter-
flies are minutely accurate, and this splendid work,

E. Hautecœur, Phot.   Salle VII

1279. Pandolfo Malatesta praying to the Virgin. — *Fabriano.*

though as cold as metal, is luminous in colouring.
Pisanello is, perhaps, also the author of the beautiful
picture attributed to Gentile da Fabriano (1370?–1450),
representing "Pandolfo Malatesta Praying to the Virgin"

(No. 1279), in the Salle des Primitifs. This work is in need
of cleaning and has the same clear and cold colouring.
The head of Malatesta is on a dark background and is
also metallically treated. We see the same minuteness
of execution in the vegetation. The faces of the Virgin
and of the Child, with their realistic and sweet expression, are treated in a manner far surpassing all that we
know of Gentile da Fabriano.

Braun, Clement & Cie., Phot.   Salle VII

1278.   The Presentation in the Temple. — Fabriano.

Of Gentile da Fabriano Michael Angelo has most
aptly said, "Aveva la mano simile al nome" (His
hand was like his name). He was gracious, gentle
and joyous. He delighted in luminous colouring and
brilliant ornamentation and loved detail in modera-
tion. His predella, "The Presentation in the Temple"
(No. 1278), shows his style to have been influenced by
that of the fourteenth century rather than by the advanced Florentine manner of his own period. The principal feature, the High Priest with the Child in his arms,
placed between the Virgin, St. Joseph, and St. Anne,
under a hexagonal kiosk, almost becomes secondary to
the accessories in the shape of two women of quality on

the left, two beggars on the right and the background with
its carefully executed architecture.

We find the same characteristics in the four pictures
of Gentile's school (Nos. 1280 to 1283), the manner of
which very nearly resembles that of the master. They
are all painted by the same hand, as is proved by the
multitude of scenes represented in the different parts of
the picture They have the same freshness of colouring,
the same attention to accessory incidents, the same
minuteness of execution in the garments, and the same
richness of ornamentation There is no inclination to
the grandiose, but there is the inherent tendency to return to primitive art peculiar to Siena which characterised and united the local schools of Umbria.

Like Fabriano, the other cities of Umbria, such as Ca-
merino, San Severino and Urbino, were uninfluenced by
the great Florentine movement The same applies to
Foligno where Nicolo Alunno (1430?–1492?) flourished

This forerunner of Perugino was acquainted with the
great works of his time, but could not assimilate them,
as is shown by the predella in three parts, in the Long
Gallery (No. 1120), representing three scenes from the
passion. The panel on the extreme left tells us that
"Nicolo Alunno painted this work in 1482 by order
of Brigida." The two angels with Umbrian features
have been draped after the manner of Ghirlandajo,
though not very successfully, for there is no breaking up
of detail in the large folds of their garments. This artifice remained unknown to Nicolo Alunno. In "The
Prayer in the Garden of Olives" (part of this predella),
the figure of Christ is eclipsed, according to the Umbri-

an manner, by the landscape and by the sleeping Apostles. In "The Flagellation" a foreign element has been introduced in the treatment of the nude, for Alunno was here influenced by the powerful genius of Signorelli, an influence which has lent life to the figures, though they are too large. A beautiful perspective has been given to the landscape by means of a serpentine road. Alunno's drawing is stiff, as we see in the "Christ on the Way to Calvary" where the horses appear to be made of wood and the cross is too long. In another panel of the predella, "The Crucifixion," the concentrated expressions and the positions of St. John and the Virgin make us realize that Nicolo Alunno was the real precursor of Perugino.

In the works of Pietro Perugino (1446–1524), we see no longer the severe grandeur of Ghirlandajo; the somewhat rude Florentine realism is modified, and there is deeper feeling. He was first taught by Piero della Francesca and was afterwards, with Lionardo and Lorenzo di Credi, under the instruction of Verrocchio He was one of the first in the Italian schools who was a complete master in the technique of painting in oils.

What he learned under these different masters was harmoniously blended with his strong personal genius and was, especially, applied to religious subjects. It was in this field that he could reveal all the peculiar qualities of his talent, as in "The Virgin and Child" (No. 1564), in the Long Gallery, — an admirable picture, painted in the year 1491. On a throne in the middle of a terrace the Virgin is seated in full face between St. Rose and St. Catherine, with the Infant Jesus on her knee. On the

E. Hautecœur, Phot.   Salle VI

1564. The Virgin and Child. — Perugino.

balustrade behind the Virgin, two angels, standing with
joined hands, are observing her with reverence. However simple the composition may, at first sight, appear,
one sees that it is the result of careful study when
one examines it attentively. The water-colour treatment gives to the work a certain hardness. All the
strength of the colouring is in the red of the Virgin's
garments, the blending of which, with the similar colour
in the robes of the two holy women, gives a great unity,

to the group in the foreground. In this luminous framing the mother supports the figure of the Child, so
white and soft and so delicately rounded. The Child
rests on the right knee of the Virgin who leans her head
to the opposite side, thus giving balance to the composition. We here see the type of woman created by Pietro
Perugino in all its purity. The face is rather broad, the
lips are tightly closed, a high, straight forehead is en-
circled by hair parted in the middle and twisted in large
curls hanging in parallel lines. The space between the
Virgin and the holy women is filled with the figures of
two angels, and their wings quite naturally conform to the
circumference of the picture, justifying its round shape.
The same applies to the curves of the arms of St Rose
and St. Catherine, the lines of which are parallel with
the framing. A wide, silvery landscape, studded with
isolated trees, opens out in the background, and this
with its distant blue mountains and green fields helps to
emphasize the depth of the composition. The balustrade
which surrounds the group breaks up the distance and
causes the foreground to appear nearer to us.

This work already shows us a gentle and tender depth
of expression unknown before and was destined to make
a profound impression on Florence and to be much appreciated in that city, agitated at the time by the violent
preaching of Savonarola.

Perugino was a stranger to grandeur, but he expressed
tenderness of feeling in a masterly manner. His "St.
Sebastian" (No. 1566 A), also in the Long Gallery, to
which the oil treatment gives an intense brilliancy, was
formerly the property of Prince Sciarra and belongs to

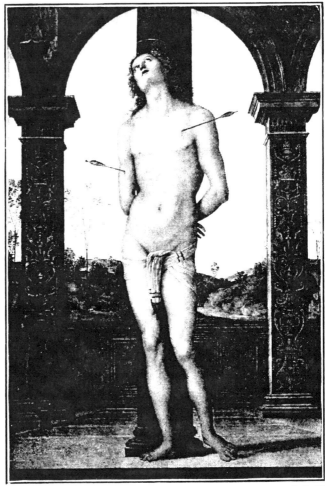

Salle VI

1566 A.   Saint Sebastian. — Perugino.

about the same period as the last picture.   It is not
pain nor ecstasy which we see in the features of the saint,
but an almost joyful suffering.   The eyes, languidly raised
to heaven, seem to express absolute resignation and sub-
mission to the will of God.   The beautiful young figure
stands out against the dark column to which it is

fastened, in the middle of an open *Renaissance* peristyle, with a far-reaching and cheerful landscape in the background.

The martyrdom of St. Sebastian was a favourite subject with the artists of the *Renaissance*, for it was the first opportunity which had presented itself for painting the nude in sacred subjects. This subject was also treated by Mantegna in a picture now in the Vienna Museum, but with the most daring realism, the figure of the young man in chains being convulsed with pain. The "St. Sebastian" by Botticelli, in Berlin, notwithstanding the excellent modelling and the graceful attitude, is but a study of the nude.

Perugino was called to Rome by Cardinal della Rovera, afterwards Julius II. Perousa entrusted him with the great work of painting the mural decoration of the Cambio, and offers of employment came from all sides. Thus, Perugino ceased to paint and began, so to speak, to manufacture pictures. Assisted by numerous companions, he repeated himself in former well-known subjects, and his execution became more and more trivial, that which was originally sentiment degenerating into a stereotyped mannerism.

"The Holy Family" (No. 1565) dates from the beginning of this change. Here there is the same gentle and lifelike treatment as in "The Virgin and Child" already mentioned. The Virgin and Child are placed, in the same manner, between St. Joseph and St. Catherine, but the feeling portrayed in his former pictures is lacking here. The faces are empty, and the picture lacks something which cannot be expressed in words. If we consider this evolution in the art of Perugino, we are tempted to believe that he had become an irreligious man. The works of his first period were painted with love and showed more than mere skill, for Perugino put all that he felt into them. But we easily perceive that this feeling

E. Hauteceur, Phot.   Salle VI

1567.   The Combat between Love and Chastity. — Perugino.

is wanting in his later works, the love of gain urging him to work with an increasing thoughtlessness and rapidity. Even the sarcasm of the young Michael Angelo could not put a stop to this falling off.

This deterioration is strikingly shown in "The Combat between Love and Chastity" (No. 1567), painted in 1505 for Elizabeth of Este, Duchess of Mantua. This abstract subject was chosen by the duchess herself and the treatment was in water-colour which was not to the liking of Perugino. The surface seems bare and the nude figures become white spots and are crowded together in a disagreeable manner. There is no question of composition, properly speaking, and the faces are without expression; the attitudes are quite conventional and sometimes borrowed, as, for instance, that of the person standing on the left which has evidently been copied from the frescoes of Signorelli.

In 1507, Pope Julius II called Perugino to Rome a second time, to decorate the Papal Palace, and the work he did there would have been afterwards removed had it not been for the reverence of Raphael for his master. The period of Perugino's greatness was gone. The "St. Paul" (No. 1566) is a work in his latest manner. The traditional type of face has lost all expression, the eyes are fixed, the garments hang clumsily on the shoulders like a coverlet on a couch, and, in the uncertainty of the features, we see the feeble and trembling hand of an old man. At the dawn of the splendid art of the sixteenth century, Perugino was a mere wreck, but he had certainly helped to prepare for its development.

The pictures of his school in the Louvre are only of moderate value, such as "The Dead Christ" (No. 1568), "The Stigmatisation of St. Francis" (No. 1569) and "St. Jerome in the Desert" (No. 1570), as well as Nos. 1571, 1572 and 1573. The first of these works lacks life and is overdrawn and full of mannerism.[6]

Bernardino Betti (1454–1513), surnamed Il Pinturicchio, a friend of Raphael, may also be counted among the pupils of Perugino. An imitator rather than an originator, he had talent for decoration and shone by the richness of ornamentation and profusion of gilding. His bad drawing he concealed by means of drapery. "The Virgin

E. Hautecœur, Phot.   Salle VI

1417.   The Virgin and Child. — *Pinturicchio.*

and Child, St. Gregory and another Saint" (No. 1417) is a good specimen of his manner and shortcomings.

The art of Perugino with its character of sweetness was bound to degenerate the moment Perugino could no longer work himself. In order to maintain its excellence it was necessary to introduce some foreign elements. This was done by Spagna (?–1530 ?) who got his training from assisting Perugino and who also assimilated the characteristics of Raphael, Pinturicchio, Ghirlandajo and even Filippo Lippi. "The Virgin and Child" (No. 1540), by Spagna, as well as an almost identical copy of it (No.

E. Hautecœur, Phot.   Salle VI

1540.   The Virgin and Child. — Spagna.

1573 A) in the Salle des Primitifs, recalls some characteristics of Raphael, especially in the faces, although they are less refined.[7] The similar inclination toward the right of the Virgin and the Child shows a remarkable absence of feeling for symmetry. The copy (No.

1573A), above mentioned, bears no name, but it can only
be by Spagna himself, although it has been attributed to
Perugino.   Compare, in both pictures, the treatment of
the landscape with the single trees on either side, the

E. Hautecœur, Phot.   Salle VI

1372.   The Virgin in Glory. — Manni.

similar inclination of the heads of the Virgin and the
Child and, above all, the position of the fingers of the Virgin's right hand.

Giannicola Manni (died 1544) followed the manner of
his master Perugino and with it incorporated that of sev-

eral other artists. In his large picture, "The Virgin in Glory" (No. 1372), in the Long Gallery, we feel the influence of Perugino. The landscape is entirely bor-

Salle VI

1607.   *St. John of Capistran.* — *Vivarini.*

rowed from him, and the face of the Virgin is but an imitation of Perugino's type. The other foreign elements in the picture are taken from Verrocchio, and his influence may also be seen in "The Baptism of Christ" (No. 1369), particularly in the composition of the central group. The male figures recall those of Raphael, and the angels those of Perugino. In "The Adoration of the Magi" (No. 1371), in the Salle des Primitifs, the treatment of the Infant Jesus is inspired by Lionardo.

Unlike Florence Venice presented no particular artistic activity at this period. Its powerful nobility were concerned with foreign affairs and held the great mass of the people in subjection. New ideas made their way only slowly, and there was no intellectual movement in its society. The spirit of the Middle Ages lasted longer in Venice than in any other part of Italy, and Byzantine art, therefore, survived here up to an advanced period in the sixteenth century. The School of Murano produced the Vivarinis and Crivellis, but these masters represented an exhausted and dead art rather than any new development.

Bartolommeo Vivarini's (?–1500?) "Portrait of St. John of Capistran" (No. 1607) shows the figure of the saint standing out against a dark background. There is almost over-refinement in the treatment of the small face and pinched lips, in the slightly inclined body and in the manner of holding the standard. The same criticism applies to "St. Bernard" (No. 1268), by Carlo Crivelli (1430–1493), painted in water-colours and executed in a masterly manner. The beautiful picture, "The Virgin and Child Adored by Angels" (No 1676 A), in which the Virgin presents the Child to two angels, is wrongly attributed by some critics to Crivelli.

ANTONELLO DA MESSINA TO LIONARDO DA VINCI

THE most important moment in the evolution of Venetian art, perhaps of Italian art in general, is that of the appearance of Antonello da Messina (1444 ?–1493), for it was he who first introduced into Italy the method of painting in oils. He left the city of Messina, which was so fertile in artistic production, to emigrate to Rome and thence to Flanders, where he became a pupil of Roger van der Weyden, and was, probably, the first Italian to succeed in mastering the process of painting in oils. This treatment satisfied his intense appreciation of colour and minuteness of execution. He was a stranger to the deep feeling required for religious subjects, but, as a daring realist and one endowed with remarkable quickness of observation, he became, on his arrival in Venice, the leading portrait painter of the time.

"The Portrait of a Man" (No. 1134), the highest manifestation of his powerful work, has a predominating warm brown shade, and the execution is of a careful minuteness without being overdone and without any trace of the brush obtruding disagreeably. The young man in this picture, with his big, defiant under-lip, has an expression of energy and grandeur that has been surpassed only by the portraits of Jan van Eyck. The artist has grasped the most subtle details of nature. All the delicate qualities which can be produced by painting in oils are represented here

1134. Portrait of a Man. — Messina.

in the fine modelling, the strong relief, the blending and transparency of the shading and the perfect treatment of the fur and tissue of the garments. The influence of Mantegna and Piero della Francesca prevented Antonello da Messina from maintaining the highest standard, as is shown by his works in the Museums of Vienna and Berlin. The process which he had brought from Flanders soon became the common property of the artists of Venice where Murano had been succeeded by the Bellinis.

Gentile Bellini (1426–1507), the elder of the two brothers, was a daring realist, while Giovanni (1428–1516) was a poet full of sentiment and feeling, one brother thus supplying qualities which the other lacked. Like true Venetians, they both had an intense love of colour. An example of the manner of Gentile Bellini is the "Portrait of

1156.   Portrait of Two Men. — Gentile Bellini.

Two Men" (No. 1156), by some follower, though attributed on the frame of the picture to Gentile Bellini himself, and to Cariani by Crowe and Cavalcaselle. Here the cheeks are flat, the hair appears artificial, and the portrait cannot be compared to that of Messina, although the expression of the eyes is full of life and character. Notwithstanding the close resemblance of these two figures which were for a long time supposed to be the Bellini brothers themselves, we discern, in the one on the left, a nature full of fire, and, in the other, a calmer temperament. We

get a better impression from Giovanni Bellini's picture, the
"Portrait of a Man" (No. 1158 A), recently acquired by the
Louvre, which hangs on the left of the Long Gallery near
the "Portrait of a Man" (No. 1134)   His gift of representing character is triumphantly displayed in this person-
age with dark hair.   Here is not a portrait only, but a
representation of the times.   His power as a colorist is
revealed by the manner in which he introduces a blue sky
and white clouds as a background and thus relieves and
almost destroys the first impression of darkness given
by the picture.

In 1479, Gentile, who was then occupied with the decoration of the great hall of the Ducal Palace, was sent by
the Republic of Venice to the Court of the Sultan Mahomet
II.   From this journey to the East, the first, perhaps, in
the annals of art, new inspirations were acquired, and
"The Reception of a Venetian Ambassador at Cairo"
(No. 1157), attributed by Mr. Berenson to Catena (1475–
1531), was the result.   At the entrance to a high gate,
seated on his divan and surrounded by his emirs, the
Sultan is receiving the ambassador of the Republic.   The
contrast between the black costume of the ambassador
and the variously coloured robes of the Orientals is very
striking.   The persons on horseback and on camels give
life to the scene, and the treatment of the perspective with
its minarets and palms is excellent.   A dazzling light
bathes the whole composition and plays in big rays upon
the arcade of the porch, producing vigorous contrasts
of light and shade.

The poetic and distinguished manner of Giovanni
Bellini is very superior to the realism of his elder brother

1157.   *Reception of a Venetian Ambassador at Cairo.* — *Gentile Bellini.*

Gentile. His domain was religious subjects In "The Virgin and Child between St. Peter and St Sebastian" (No. 1158),³ there is a gentle repose on the face of the Virgin, and, though there is nothing divine about her, she is full of poetic charm. The handsome St. Sebastian clasps his hands in timid veneration, and St. Peter holds the key in an energetic manner Resolution is printed upon Peter's features, and we are reminded of the words addressed to him "Thou art Peter and upon this rock I will build my church" In the lighter tints of the picture, Giovanni shows himself to be a great colourist, as, for instance, in the white of the cloak and veil of the Virgin, in the figures of the Child and St. Sebastian and in the white clouds in which float the heads of angels.

Of the numerous imitators of Giovanni Bellini, however faithful their imitation, none could equal his excellence, for with them tranquillity became indifference, and sweetness, vapidity. This is shown in "The Virgin and Child with St. Sebastian" (No. 1159), a picture of his school which, although it does not lack charm, has not the power nor the colouring of Giovanni

Gentile Bellini, before his death in 1507, had confided to his brother Giovanni the completion of his work, "The Preaching of St. Mark," now in Milan. From this, the picture in the Louvre called "The Preaching of St. Stephen in Jerusalem" (No. 1211), by Vittorio Carpaccio (died 1518?), is entirely borrowed. The composition of the two is almost identical St. Stephen stands on a high pedestal at the left surrounded by a group of listeners many of whom wear Oriental costumes, and the background is full of cupolas, minarets and pleasant green hills. But that which Carpaccio could not imitate was the dazzling sun of the south. In spite of his efforts to give an impression of it, he could not prevent his colouring from being somewhat yellow and grey.

The new process of oil painting which Antonello da Mes-

E. Hautecœur, Phot.   Salle VI

1211.   The Preaching of St. Stephen at Jerusalem. — Carpaccio.

sina had introduced into Venice was improved upon by the Bellini brothers who collected about them artists of diverse characteristics. One of the most agreeable of these was Cima da Conegliano (died 1517?), a master par excellence of religious subjects. The grouping in his picture, " The Virgin and Infant Jesus" (No. 1259), is strictly pyramidal. The Virgin looks with devotion upon the Infant Jesus

who rests upon her knees, while two saints approach and
adore Him. Their positions, though graceful, are somewhat affected. Behind the Virgin is a large, richly decorated canopy, a detail for which the Venetian artists had a
predilection, and which Albrecht Dürer also introduced
into German art. In the distance stretches out a beautiful
landscape representing a country scene of Frioul, the inspiration of which we owe to the love of the artist for his
native land. Here winds a silvery river, while bright fields
and the frowning tower of a fortified castle, all richly
warm in colouring, make a singularly beautiful background
in the picture.

Andrea Mantegna (1431–1506), son of a poor peasant,
was adopted at the age of ten by Francesco Squarcione
who taught the art of embroidery as well as painting.
Moreover, Squarcione, like a modern master, made his
pupils work from plaster models of the antique, and Mantegna thus became enamoured of the forms of antiquity
which afterwards inspired all his works. But art was still
too much in its infancy for any danger to come from purely
academical work. Mantegna's character was too realistic
and decided to fall under the influence of archaism. He
was one of the greatest artists of his time and was the
first who, keeping truth ever in sight, introduced into
painting all the elements of antique forms and infused
into them his own peculiar spirit.

From this point of view let us consider one of his first
works, "Calvary" (No. 1373). This picture shows all
the characteristics of his manner — realistic treatment,
knowledge of perspective and the introduction of elements
from the antique. From a paved surface rise three crosses,

and, on the central one, Christ is nailed between those bearing the two thieves. On the right are some soldiers who, with perfect indifference, throw dice for the Saviour's garments while others, on horseback, with equal indifference, raise their eyes to the cross. On the left are St. John,

E. Hautecœur, Phot.   Salle VI

1373.   Calvary. — Mantegna.

bathed in tears, and the Virgin who is only prevented from sinking by the support of some holy women. A steep road leads to Jerusalem on a height in the background. The composition is strong. The cross of the Saviour is placed in the open space between two mountains, thus causing it to stand out from those of the two thieves which are less in relief against their darker background. The deep, wide landscape, the steepness of the road leading up to the town,

the softness of the tones paling in colour and vanishing
in the distance constitute a very realistic perspective. But
the picture's most striking feature is its truth of expression
and action. The Roman legions have the classic calm of
figures in antique bas-reliefs, in striking contrast to the
group in which we see the Virgin. On her aged face there
is an expression of distracted grief Her arms fall inert,
her body is inanimate, and her face is of a paleness as
death-like as that of the body of her Son.

Mantegna was called by the Duke Ludovico Gonzaga
(1460) to Mantua, where he painted the series of frescoes
in the "camera degli sposi" (bridal chamber) of the old
castle.

On the death of Gonzaga, Mantegna devoted his services
to the Duke's son, Francesco, and in "The Virgin of the
Victory" (No. 1374), painted in 1496, he transformed into
a victory the defeat which this prince had suffered at the
hands of Charles VIII of France. In this picture the
Virgin is seated under a canopy of foliage richly ornamented with garlands, and blesses the Child whom she
holds standing on her knees. Her cloak is held by the
Archangel Michael and St. George who spread it out in
the form of a canopy. By her side stands St John the
Baptist and, in the background, we see St Andrew and
St. Longinus The composition is in the form of a perfect pyramid, and, from the summit of the construction,
there hangs a branch of coral The drawing is excellent,
and the composition, owing to the manner in which the
persons are bound to one another by the cloak of the Virgin, and to the way in which the figures of Francesco
and St. Elizabeth are introduced, is masterly. The

Salle VI

1374.   The Virgin of the Victory.—Mantegna.

scheme of colour is even superior to the drawing. A certain unity of tone is given by the red garment of the Virgin, the head-dress of St. Longinus and the branch of coral, and red is scattered here and there in the rich garlands which are like painted Roman bas-reliefs. It is a work which has been carefully thought out in all its harmonious details and unites and combines the characteristics of ancient and modern art

Mantegna had the good fortune, which few enjoy, to maintain the same high level up to old age, although that old age was not exempt from cares. This excellence is shown in two mythological pictures painted in the last years of his life.

Elizabeth of Este, who ordered one of these, herself chose the subject "The Victory of Virtue over Vice" (No. 1376). Minerva, armed with a lance and preceded by two nymphs, is seen to burst from a wood; at sight of her the Vices fly, and among them, Venus, represented as standing on the back of a centaur. The Virtues, in their turn, appear in a halo of clouds. An inscription on the figure on the left is intended to make this poetic fable intelligible. Andrea Mantegna knew how to make the most of this ungrateful subject. The figure of Venus contributes the perpendicular effect which gives equilibrium to the picture. The dominant lines, on the left, pass over Minerva and are directed towards the fluttering cupids, while a descending curve, on the opposite side, is formed by figures carrying Avarice and Ingratitude. The picture is painted in water colours, a process requiring particular care, in which Mantegna excelled and to which he remained faithful all his life.

"Parnassus" (No. 1375), is an even superior work. On a natural eminence of rocks, Mars is taking leave of Venus and, below, the Nine Muses are dancing to the music of Apollo's lyre. On the right is Mercury leaning on Pega-

E. Hautecœur, Phot.   Salle VI

1376.   Victory of Virtue over Vice. — Mantegna.

sus and, from the top of the rocks, Cupid blows a pipe at Vulcan in his forge. Until Raphael, Italian art never displayed so much charm and so much grace of movement as is found here. The pose of each Muse is different from that of the rest, and yet they are all equally graceful. These figures, drawn from the antique, far from being painted statues, seem instinct with life. Mars and Venus form a group of statuesque beauty. The landscape, which we see through a vista, with its blue mountains and green fields, is worthy of being the abode of the gods. The whole is bathed in a bright light, the dazzling body of Venus

E. Hautecœur, Phot.   Salle VI

1375.   Parnassus. — Mantegna.

stands out against a background of dark green, and, in the gloomy cavern of Vulcan, we see the gleam of his red cloak.

When Mantegna died at Mantua, in 1506, the art of Mantua died with him, but his influence remained and dominated all Northern Italy. This influence may be seen in the "Ecce Homo" (No. 1393) by Bartolommeo Montagna of Vicenza (died 1523?), who followed in his footsteps.

Montagna also shows himself to have been influenced by the Bellinis, as may be seen in the agreeable picture called "Three Young Musicians" (No. 1394).

Salle VI

1318.   The Virgin and Child. — Attributed to Girolamo dai Libri.

The school of Verona also was affected by Andrea Mantegna, and this is evident in a picture called "The Virgin and Child" (No. 1318) attributed to Girolamo dai Libri, (1474–1556) but which might better be attributed to Carotto

in whom the characteristics of the art of Mantua are strongly mingled with Venetian influences.[9] This exchange, this
"traffic" of ideas between
these two artistic centres is
one of the most interesting of
studies. A characteristic of
the school of Verona is the
very rich, light colouring
which clearly distinguishes it
from the Venetian School.

In Lombardy, the influ-
ence of Mantegna was greatly
attenuated by local characteristics. These consisted in a
certain calm, a certain sweetness of expression peculiar to
the works which preceded
Lionardo, as, for example,
in the case of Borgognone
(1450–1523). In his "Presentation in the Temple" (No.
1181), the faces, although
natural and animated, have
a severely mute expression.

E. Hautecœur, Phot.   Salle VI

*1182 A. St. Augustine and a
Donor. — Borgognone.*

With the Virgin, emotion is
under control; and, in the
Child, it is only expressed by
an attitude of affection. In the two neighboring portraits,
"St. Peter of Verona and an Unknown Woman" (No.
1182) and "St. Augustine and a Donor" (No. 1182 A),
notwithstanding the pains taken in the execution, the

pleasing impression left by their better qualities is spoiled
by the grey tint of the faces.   This greyish tint is again
found in Bartolommeo Suardi il Bramantino (died 1530).
His "Circumcision" (No 1545) is dark in tone, and there
is again the same expression of calm and inward devotion
in the face of the Virgin, while the livid and aged man
on the right reminds us of the "Presentation in the
Temple" (No. 1181) by Borgognone.

Piero Francesco Sacchi di Pavia (after 1527), author of
the "Four Fathers of the Church" (No. 1488), is generally
an indifferent master, but appears to us here to good advantage.   The psychological characteristics of each figure
are carefully studied.   On the left is St. Gregory, the
man of unshakable and blind faith, with the Scriptures
open before him.   Next is St. Augustine, the philosopher,
listening to and writing down what the Holy Ghost, in
the form of a Dove, is communicating to him   Then
comes St. Jerome, in ecstasy turning to the angel.   Finally
we see St. Ambrose mending his pen, and by his calmness
and simplicity he forms a decided contrast to the others.
The colouring is light, the execution of the details is careful
without being overdone, and the wide blue landscape is
imposing.

To the Lombard school at this remote period belonged
likewise two masters, both of whom had little charm.
The one, Fasoli, called Lorenzo di Pavia, who died about
1520(?), crowded too many figures into his picture called
"The Family of the Holy Virgin" (No. 1284), thus producing a medley of heads and limbs.   The grouping of
the other, Bartolommeo Bononi, who painted at the beginning of the sixteenth century, is good in his picture

E. Hautecœur, Phot.   Salle VI

1488.   Four Fathers of the Church. — Sacchi.

called "The Virgin and Child" (No. 1174), but the colouring is weak and reminds us of a chromo-lithograph.

The manner of the school of Ferrara is quite the opposite of that of the peaceful and gentle school of Milan. At
Ferrara the old Cosimo Tura (1432–1495), called Cosmè.
is the initiator of a severe school. In his "Pietà" (No.

1556), there is no trace of composition properly speaking. The emaciation of the body of Christ, which rests on the Virgin's knees, is so distinct as to cause it to resemble a skeleton. The faces contracted by grief have nothing pleasing, and the action is exaggerated. But, nevertheless, there is great power in this work and a daring and

E. Hautecœur, Phot.   Salle VI

1556.   Pietà. — Cosimo Tura.

conscious realism.   The picture is painted in water-colours, but the colouring is as crude as enamel, and the hues are inharmoniously juxtaposed. The folds of the drapery are too fine and abruptly broken up, and the shadows are too strong. The same applies to his "Portrait of a Saint" (No. 1557).

Another example of the hard style of the primitive school of Ferrara is the small picture called "The Virgin and Child" (No. 1523), attributed, probably wrongly, to Gregorio de Schiavone.[10] The colours are loud and shine like lacquer. The heads are ugly, and the drapery is as stiff as metal. The St. Apollonia and St. Michael in the pictures Nos. 1677 A and B are also in this manner, but there is a modification showing a transition between

E. Hautecœur, Phot.   Salle VI

1523. The Virgin and Child. — Attributed to Gregorio de Schiavone.

Cosimo Tura and his pupil, Lorenzo Costa (1460–1535), the most agreeable artist of the school of Ferrara, who was one of the first to discover the secret beauties of nature. His natural gentleness counterbalanced the severe manner

of his master. He readily assimilated foreign elements
and was inspired by the school of Bologna, where Francia
was his companion, and by that of Mantua where he came
under the strong influence of Mantegna.

Salle VI

1261.   The Court of Isabella of Este. — Lorenzo Costa.

All this we see in one of Costa's most attractive creations
painted at an advanced age, "The Court of Isabella of
Este" (No. 1261). Here we have an excellent landscape
with a moist atmosphere and dark trees. On the glistening water floats a galley, and there is an expanse of green
grass, the different levels of which are skilfully used as elements of composition. Grouped upon it in a semicircle

are persons writing or playing music, a woman armed with
a bow, and a slayer of dragons In the middle distance
is Isabella who is being crowned by a cupid In front are
seated two beautiful young girls Only the colouring and
preference for red and strong blues recall the manner of
Cosimo Tura. Isabella's inclined and inert attitude
is borrowed from Francia, while the slayer of dragons
is taken from Mantegna. That which peculiarly belongs to Costa in this picture is the charming and velvety
quality of the landscape, denoting his passionate love for
the beautiful in nature [11] This is one more example of the
richness arising from the association of several influences.

A still more remarkable example of this kind is the
picture by Domenico Panetti (died 1512), "The Nativity"
(No. 1401), in Salle IX, opening from the Long Gallery.
This, by its enamel-like brilliancy of colour and by the
hardness of the drawing again shows the manner of the
school of Ferrara, but, in its type of face and, above all,
in the simple and careful interpretation of the landscape,
it shows the influence of the schools of Bologna and
of Francia.

Francesco Raibolini, called Il Francia (1450–1517), before he became a painter, had commenced his career as a
jeweller and engraver. But it seems as if the hardness of
metal was incompatible with the sweetness of his temperament, for he turned to painting, bringing to it the scrupu-
lous precision and distinctness of detail which he borrowed
from the exercise of his first art. He was inspired by
Mantegna, and many of his ideas were similar to those
of Costa, but he had a depth of feeling unknown to these
two artists. One may call him the master of movement

and gesture. In his "Christ on the Cross" (No. 1436) there is grief and despair in the inclined position, and in the expression and gesture. The tense position of the hands and body of St. John and the inertness of the arms of the

Braun, Clement & Cie., Phot.   Salle IX

1401.   The Nativity. — Panetti.

Virgin indicate the same emotion in both. But the figure of Joseph lying at the foot of the cross is distorted and not pleasing. The dark cross, on which the paleness of the body of Christ stands out in relief, is very effective. The colours are, moreover, brilliant, and the shadows strongly marked.

The intensity of Perugino and the sentiment of Francia

E. Hautecœur, Phot.   Salle VI

1436.   Christ on the Cross. — Francia.

were too closely allied not to influence each other recipro-
cally.   Traces of this influence are to be seen in Francia's
small picture called "The Nativity" (No. 1435) where the
face of the Virgin bears very characteristic traces of the manner of Perugino.   Francia was not to lose his own peculiar

manner, however. "The Virgin and Child with a Hermit" (No. 1437) is a genuine and good example of his style, but was not painted by him. The colours are brilliant and the action spirited. The expression of gen-

E. Hautecœur, Phot.   Salle VI

1437.   The Virgin and Child. — By a Pupil of Francia.

tle earnestness on the face of the hermit and the broadly treated landscape are certainly in his manner.

To the school of Francia belongs the pleasing picture called "The Virgin and Child Surrounded by Saints" (No. 1436 A). The Virgin is seated on a throne before a curtain stretched between two columns. The Child

is exquisitely natural and leans toward St. John the
Baptist, and quite in the foreground is St. Francis. On
the other side St. Sebastian, with ecstatically raised eyes,
leans against a column, while in front of him is St. George
in armour, and at the feet of the Virgin an angel plays on

E. Hautecœur, Phot.   Salle IX ·

1381.   Christ carrying the Cross. — Marchesi.

a musical instrument.   Although this work is weak in colouring, it is, on the other hand, very sympathetic, owing
to its sweetness of expression and its excellent composition.   The inclined position of the Child binds the central
group most naturally to that on the side.   Naturalness and
strength in the figures are observable throughout the picture; on one side are the ascetic St. John the Baptist and
St. Francis in a more or less careless position; on the other

are the graceful St. Sebastian and beside him the energetic St. George. We have here a work presenting all the features of the sixteenth century art.

Thus the characteristics of the art of the sixteenth century also penetrated the schools of Ferrara and Bologna, and in the latter place they were fully developed by Giro-

E. Hautecœur, Phot.   Salle VI

1384.   The Nativity. — Massone.

lamo Marchesi (1480?–1550), a pupil of Francia, and author of "Christ Carrying the Cross" (No. 1381), in Salle IX. We see here an expression of acute grief in the features of the Saviour, and this is a masterly work of perfect technique.

Two pictures claim our attention which are somewhat outside the evolution which we have just been studying. One by Giovanni Massone, a picture in three parts called "The Nativity, with Pope Sixtus and Cardinal Giuliano della Rovera" (No. 1384), was painted towards the end of the fifteenth century, and shows that, in architecture and in painting, the Piedmontese felt the strong influence of Mantegna. But the predominance of dark tints which makes this picture sombre shows it to be of the school of Lombardy. The other picture, "The Annunciation" (No. 1676), an altar screen the colouring of which is entirely light, seems, by the profusion of its gilded ornamentation as well as by its background consisting of a landscape of Italian fields, to belong to an unknown local school, perhaps that of Genoa.

We now reach the greatest epoch in the history of art, and the first master among its exponents was Lionardo da Vinci.

LIONARDO TO RAPHAEL

IN Lionardo da Vinci (1452–1519) every talent was combined in one man. All that humanity had up to that time produced constituted the foundation of his genius. His works are still, to-day, an enigma from the point of view of treatment. His great mind seemed to solve all problems. As a military engineer, he made plans of fortifications which are still modern. He conceived the power of steam and even constructed flying machines But he produced little because even perfection did not satisfy him. He was born at Vinci in 1452 and was a natural son of the notary Ser Pier At an early age he was admitted to the studio of Verrocchio, and the angels which, as pupil, he painted into Verrocchio's picture, "The Baptism of Christ," show an incomparable superiority over the work of his master.

Lionardo remained in Florence till 1485 and then entered the service of Ludovico il Moro in Milan, where he spent fourteen happy years, universally admired as a man, a sculptor, a naturalist and a painter. The downfall of the Sforzas threw him into a changing and agitated existence. He first went to Venice, where he remained till 1503, thence to Romagna under Cæsar Borgia, afterwards to Florence in 1506, next to Rome, and from there back again to Milan. In 1507 he entered the service of Francis I, but only settled permanently in France in 1516, and here he remained up to the time of his death which took

place in the Chateau Cloux at Amboise in the year 1519.
Ill health during the last part of his life prevented him
from doing any great work for his protector and admirer,
Francis I.

There is one composition which the name of Lionardo
recalls to all minds, a work equalled in renown only by
"The Sistine Madonna" of Raphael. This is "The Last

E. Hautecœur, Phot.   Salle VI

1603. The Last Supper. — Copy by Oggiono of Lionardo's painting in Milan.

Supper," in Milan. What we possessed of the original at
Milan was at best scarcely more than a ruin, and has, of
late, entirely perished. Lionardo's experiments in the
mixture of oils, which in this instance proved to be
perishable, in addition to damages from the vandalism
which transformed into a stable and granary the hall in
which the picture was painted, have resulted ultimately
in its utter destruction and, for this reason, the value of
contemporary copies have become of singular importance. The copy in the Louvre (No. 1603), by Marco
Oggiono, in the Long Gallery, is an example of this.

The moment represented in this picture is the one in which Christ has just said, "One of you will betray Me," and in the midst of the agitation which these words provoke, the Master is the only one who remains calm. On either side, without laboured effect, are two groups, each of three Apostles.   Christ thus becomes the centre of the picture and stands out in relief against the landscape in the background.   Judas and St. John are united in the same group and thus form a striking contrast.   The various positions of the heads are very remarkable.   Christ is in full face, the figures at the extremities of the table are in profile, while the perpendicular walls allow us to appreciate the attitudes of the figures.   The hands are full of character. Christ appears to be saying: "So has My Father decreed: let His Will be done"   Judas grasps his purse, St. John gently joins his hands, while St. James, on the contrary, opens his wide, as if saying· "Master, it is not possible." The greatness of this work consists in that we understand the scene without effort.   Lionardo's "Last Supper" differs essentially from all preceding creations, and all those who have since attempted this subject have been inspired by it.

"The Virgin of the Rocks" (No. 1599) is a composition truly in the style of Lionardo and consists of a triangular group in the centre of which is the Virgin.   We here see, for the first time, the harmonious blending of figures in the midst of an unusual landscape.   Under projecting rocks on the edge of a pool, the Virgin and an angel watch the Infant Jesus as he blesses St. John, who raises his hands as if in prayer.   The wild and rocky landscape seems to belong to the world of

dreams. The expression of the Virgin shows the
first appearance of that mysterious smile to which Lio-

E. Hautecœur, Phot.   Salle VI

1599.   The Virgin of the Rocks. — Lionardo.

nardo's "Monna Lisa" owes its greatest charm. As is
always the case with Lionardo, there is in the treatment of the hands an energy of expression absolutely

unknown till then, and they are a study in themselves. Certain archaic traces still remain in this work; the modelling of the bodies of the children is of a metallic clearness and recalls the manner of Verrocchio, as do the angular folds of the drapery. The last signs of fifteenth century influences appear in the bony structure of the heads. Some of these traces are also noticeable in another early work of Lionardo, "La Belle Ferronnière" (No. 1600), which is now considered by most critics to be the portrait of Lucrezia Crivelli. The freshness of youth and the thoughtful expression of the eyes exercise an irresistible attraction. Here the height of the forehead is accentuated and ornamented by a jewel attached to a narrow band of silk. (High foreheads were at that time much in fashion, and, to create this effect, women of quality were accustomed to pluck out the hair from the forehead and even from the eyebrows) The rounded body seems to breathe under the lacing of the red robe which furnishes it with a luminous setting. The oval of the face stands out a little too sharply, but this is due to the three-quarters pose. The picture No. 1605 is now held to be the portrait of La Belle Ferronnière and most certainly belongs to the school of Lionardo.

The most perfect work of art ever produced is, perhaps, Lionardo's portrait of Monna Lisa, also called "La Joconda" (No. 1601; see Frontispiece). When Lionardo separated himself from it at the end of four years' work, he declared it to be still unfinished. This work has not escaped the consequences of unfortunate technical experiments in the preparation of oils. The light tints of the skin and the brightness have disappeared, and the underlying grey

E. Hautecœur, Phot. Salle VI

1600. Portrait of Lucrezia Crivelli. — Lionardo.

coating is visible. "Let him," says Vasari, "who wishes
to know to what degree art can imitate nature, contemplate this picture. It is rather a divine work than the
work of a man." That which strikes us is the mobility
in this apparently immobile figure. Monna Lisa is seated
in a low chair on the left arm of which she leans and

lightly rests an arm; her long narrow eyes seem on the
point of languorously closing; the corners of the mouth are
a little raised, and there is a mysterious and indescribable
smile; the hands are incomparably moulded, and one may
almost feel their warmth and velvety softness. Lionardo
was the first artist who was able, in painting, to render the texture and suppleness of the skin. The hair
is delicately and carefully treated, there are half tints
on the cheeks, and a pale light reflected from the folds
of the green gown and the yellow sleeves gently touches
the hands A stone balustrade separates the figure
from the landscape and this serves to incline it, as it
were, toward the spectator, at the same time leaving
it connected with the background. Many and deep
are the distances which we see in these blue mountains, and it is a landscape of fantastic dreamland far
beyond our reach, for the little bridge is to indicate
distance and seems to lead to other worlds. Much has
already been written concerning the "Monna Lisa,"
but no one has fathomed all the enigmas of this sphinx-
like face. Walter Pater, in "The Renaissance," says
of this mystic creation. "The presence that thus rose so
strangely beside the waters, is expressive of what in the
ways of a thousand years men had come to desire. Hers
is the head upon which all 'the ends of the world are
come,' and the eyelids are a little weary. It is a beauty
wrought out from within upon the flesh, the deposit,
little cell by cell, of strange thoughts and fantastic
reveries and exquisite passions. Set it for a moment
beside one of those white Greek goddesses or beautiful women of antiquity, and how would they be

E. Hautecœur, Phot. Salle VI

1597. St. John the Baptist. — Lionardo.

troubled by this beauty, into which the soul with all
its maladies has passed! All the thoughts and experience of the world have etched and moulded there, in
that which they have of power to refine and make expressive the outward form, the animalism of Greece,
the lust of Rome, the reverie of the middle age with its

spiritual ambition and imaginative loves, the return of
the Pagan world, the sins of the Borgias. She is older
than the rocks among which she sits; like the vampire,
she has been dead many times, and learned the secrets
of the grave; and has been a diver in deep seas, and
keeps their fallen day about her; and trafficked for strange
webs with Eastern merchants." It would be unfair to
compare any other work of Lionardo or of his contemporaries with this wonderful creation.

The "St. John the Baptist" (No. 1597), which has been
attributed to Lionardo, is a picture well executed by a pupil
and is but a variation of the "Monna Lisa." The magic
smile has here become less subtle and enlarges the mouth,
and the mystery of the expression is lost. But the charm
of the skin remains and the surface vibrates with lights
which play upon and animate the modelling of the neck.
There is a tradition that a Bacchus painted by Lionardo
was brought to France at the commencement of the sixteenth century, but we cannot identify this work with the
"Bacchus" of the Louvre (No. 1602). There is too
much sameness in the movement of the hands, the left
leg rests too heavily on the right, and the treatment of the
vegetation in the foreground is almost trifling. But there
is something of the spirit of Lionardo in the brilliant look
of those open and living eyes and in the treatment of
the landscape with its mysterious depth. Though this
work is not by Lionardo, it must have been inspired by
him.

But the picture called "The Virgin, the Infant Jesus,
and St. Anne" (No. 1598), in the Salon Carré, has all the
characteristics of Lionardo. It is only in Michael Angelo

E. Hautecœur, Phot.   Salon Carré

1508.   The Virgin, the Infant Jesus and St. Anne. — Lionardo.

that we find such remarkable concentration in a composition. It would seem as if Lionardo here wished to solve the problem of grouping in a limited space. This group forms a triangle. St. Anne is entirely full face, and smiles at the Virgin seated on her lap. The Infant Jesus is engaged in childish play with a lamb which He is seizing by the ears, while He turns toward the Virgin bending above Him, as if to draw her attention to His sport. These different attitudes produce a richness of action contrasting with the vertical lines furnished by the figure of St. Anne These are, however, a little broken by reason of her bent arm and the inclined head of the Virgin. If one considers the smiles on the faces of the women and the different means employed to express maternal love, it is impossible to attribute this work to any other than Lionardo, though it unfortunately bears traces of having been left unfinished by the artist Here again we find the mysterious blue landscape and the mountains with their wild and abrupt summits similar to those in "The Virgin of the Rocks" and the "Monna Lisa."

Lionardo himself having achieved such perfection, it was impossible for his pupils and imitators to surpass or even equal him, however much they might assimilate the expression and manner of his school. Among these was Cesare da Sesto (1480–1521) "The Virgin of the Scales" (No. 1604), now known to be by Sesto, is but a variation of "The Virgin, the Infant Jesus, and St. Anne," but is lacking in construction. The Virgin, to whom an angel presents the scales, and the Child are too symmetrical. The attitude of the heads of the Mother and Child are similar and produce an awkward effect; although they are well bound together with the angel and St. John, Elizabeth is quite outside the group to the left. She is borrowed from Mantegna (see No. 1374) and here only serves as an accessory without any relation to the general scheme of the composition.

The original picture of which "The Virgin and Infant

E. Hautecœur, Phot.   Salle VI

1604.   The Virgin of the Scales. — Cesare da Sesto.

Jesus" (No. 1603 A) is an insipid Flemish copy, must
have been by one of the master's imitators and not by
Lionardo himself. As for "The Annunciation" (No.
1602 A), Mr. Berenson, with all the weight of his au-
thority, considers this a work of Lionardo's youth.

Though none of Lionardo's successors attained his

perfection, some approached it superficially. This is
the case with Marco da Oggiono (1470–1530), whose
"Virgin and Child" (No. 1382 A) is a natural and ex-

E. Hautecœur, Phot.   Salle VI

1382.   The Holy Family. — Oggiono.

pressive rendering of maternal happiness. There is
much movement and expression in the action with which
the Virgin holds and presses the Child to her.   It is from
Lionardo that this artist learned all that can be expressed

in hands and attitudes. The face, with its delicate smile, is also borrowed from Lionardo, but the colouring is colder, and the expression of the Child is not natural. His "Holy Family" (No. 1382), when compared with Lionardo's work, is again very inferior. It has more

E. Hautecœur, Phot.   Salle VI.

1169.   The Virgin of the Casio Family. — Boltraffio.

movement and is more elaborately treated, but the background is colder, the drawing and colouring are harder, and the execution is imperfect.

A second pupil of Lionardo was Gianantonio (Giovanni Antonio) Boltraffio (1467–1516) who attained a grand simplicity in "The Virgin of the Casio Family" (No. 1169). The composition consists of a simple juxtaposition of the Virgin with the two donors who are bound together by the colouring of the three different reds in the garments. The heads are remarkably natural and broadly executed. The type and attitude of the Virgin are almost those of a woman of the people, and the landscape is treated with the same splendid simplicity. Although the drawing of the hands of the Child and of the person on the left is bad, this work contrasts favourably with the then prevailing mania for prettiness only.

Thus, it was to Lionardo that all his successors turned as a source of inspiration. From him Marco da Oggiono learned pure form; Boltraffio, grandeur; and Andrea Solario (1460?–1530?), colour and a velvety treatment of the skin. The art of this last is one of the best examples of the evolution in manner which can take place during the lifetime of an artist. At first, Solario was a follower of the old Lombard school of the fifteenth century and continued so up to the time of his painting "The Crucifixion" (No. 1532), dated 1503. Here his colours are cold and have the hardness of enamel; the predominating loud red and blue on the sides do not harmonise well, and they are made still more discordant by the intense white of the cross. The faces and bodies are after the realistic school of Mantegna, but they indicate no attempt at beauty. With this compare "The Virgin of the Green Cushion" (No. 1530), a specimen of Solario's later manner, in which we see the ideal type of face created by Lionardo, with the look of intense maternal devotion. Here, also, is Lionardo's red-brown hair, expressive attitude and soft and living flesh. The Child lies in a natural position, the colours are warm, and the play of the lights and shadows is remarkable.

The "Head of St. John the Baptist on a Charger"
(No. 1533), by the same artist, is beautiful, in spite of

E. Hautecœur, Phot.   Salle VI

1532.   The Crucifixion. — Solario.

its deathlike whiteness. The red beard is carefully executed, the blood on the neck is visible, notwithstanding
the deep shadow which covers it, and the whole work is

E. Hautecœur, Phot.   Salle VI

1530.   The Virgin of the green cushion. — Solario.

remarkably treated. The "Portrait of Charles of Amboise" (No. 1531), on the other hand, with its minute execution, is hard and lifeless.

A keen sense of beauty and of something deep and mysterious principally distinguishes Bernardino Luini (1475 ?–1533 ?). Only a few of these characteristics are to be found in one of his first works, a fresco representing the "Forge of Vulcan" (No. 1356) painted for the Villa Pelucca. The god, who is forging a wing for Eros, is seated, and is lacking in character. Venus is full of

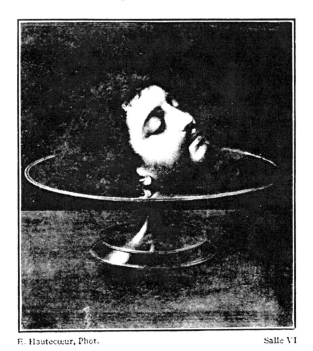

E. Hautecœur, Phot.   Salle VI

1533.   The head of John the Baptist on a charger. — Solario.

mannerism in pose and expression, and the colours are hard and indistinct. The two frescoes (Nos. 1357 and 1358) are also from the Villa Pelucca. The true Luini, with qualities reflected from Lionardo, first asserts himself in the frescoes of the Villa Litta. But Luini never had vigour in composition. The "Adoration of the Magi" (No. 1360), in Salle V, is divided into two groups by means of a large wall, and the figures thus seem too cramped in the small space. This also is to be seen in the

treatment of the background which is shallow and only
allows a glimpse into the distance. Neither was Luini a
great innovator, for the attitudes of his figures are apt
to be conventional. But he learned much from Lionardo,
and, though lacking his depth, he had his own peculiar
charm of softness and refinement. This may be seen in
the Virgin's face which quite conforms in this picture to
the type created by Lionardo with its long, delicate, oval
form, fine nose, and small mouth. The features of the
aged king belong to the old traditions of the school of
Milan, and his attitude and expression are those of profound adoration. The colouring is agreeable. The landscape, far from having the majesty of Lionardo, is an
almost idyllic scene enhanced by the descending caravan.
The same peaceful and agreeable characteristics are to
be found in "The Nativity" (No. 1359), with its carefully
treated details; but "Christ in the Act of Giving His
Blessing" (No. 1361) is too crude in its tones, and the
expression is insipid and commonplace. Luini's pupils
doubtless assisted in this work as well as in the frescoes
of "The Annunciation" (No. 1363). "A Dead Christ"
(No. 1364) and the "Curius Dentatus Refusing the Gifts
of the Samnites" (No. 1365) form part of the same series
and have much less value. The little fresco "The Head
of a Young Girl Personifying Silence" (No. 1362) leaves
a disagreeable impression owing to the bad drawing
of the finger. The expression of the face is, however,
pleasing.

If we compare Luini's treatment of "Salome Receiving the Head of St. John the Baptist" (No. 1355) with
Solario's treatment of a similar subject, we easily no-

E. Hautecœur, Phot.

1355. Salome receiving the head of John the Baptist. — Luini.

tice their distinctive characteristics. In Luini's picture,
Salome holds the charger on which a hand is placing
the bleeding head, and she is here of an original type.
The fine, elongated oval of the face and the delicate
features resemble the creations of Lionardo. The deep
shadows under the eyes make them look large and give

1353.   The Holy Family. — Luini.

them a mysterious expression. The head of St. John
best shows the difference between these two artists.
With Solario we find realism expressed by a pale,
deathlike colour and disordered hair, and there is an

expression of suffering and resignation on the features. With Luini all this is softened. The colour is pale but not deathlike, the hair is not in disorder, the expression

E. Hautecœur, Phot.   Salon Carré

1354.   The sleeping Infant Jesus. — Luini.

is peaceful, and the features express scarcely any physical pain.

In contrast to our modern search for originality, the artists of the sixteenth century reproduced again and again, without change, types which they had once adopted. Thus it was with Luini in his "Holy Family" (No. 1353).

The Virgin resembles Salome, and in St. Joseph the type
of St. John the Baptist repeats itself.

For some ten years Luini followed in the footsteps of
Lionardo, and it was not until somewhat late in life that

E. Hautecœur, Phot.   Salle VI

1285.   Saint Paul. — Ferrari.

he attempted to work on his own lines.   "The Sleeping Infant Jesus" (No. 1354) is original both in conception and treatment.   The Virgin is about to envelop
the Child, who is asleep on her arm, in a covering which
an angel spreads out before her.   In this sleeping Child,

with his head falling forward and relaxed limbs, we see natural and unaffected art The Virgin has become more womanly and no longer has the ideal features of the past, for the face is broader and less delicate, and she is entirely devoted to her maternal cares. This scene is so true and real that a woman might have been the author of it.

Thus, greater delicacy of feeling was introduced among the followers of Lionardo, and the vigorous element was modified into a sweet dreaminess. This we see in the "St. Paul" (No. 1285) by Gaudenzio Ferrari (1471 ?–1546). The Apostle is languorous, not only in expression but in attitude. The characteristics of Lionardo have almost completely disappeared, and it is only in the excellence of the drawing that we still find them. There is still a certain hardness of colouring, but another influence is at work — an influence that almost exclusively prevailed during the following centuries This new inspiration came from Raphael, who inspired the art of the sixteenth century, and whose name has become the symbol of art in general.

RAPHAEL TO THE VENETIAN SCHOOL

WITH the great trio, Lionardo, Michael Angelo, and Raphael, art attained the highest point yet reached in Italy. Of these, Raphael (1483–1520) is the most harmonious. With him there was no waste of strength in excessive universality as with Lionardo, no diversity of gifts as with the sculptor-painter-poet, Michael Angelo. Raphael was a painter only and was the most human of the three.

Lionardo was the man of feeling who surprised the most intimate mysteries of the soul, and knew how to interpret them; Michael Angelo was a Titan from another world who created a world of Titans like himself; but Raphael reveals all the incomparable beauties of this earth. He seems to have seen all things and their attributes in their perfection, and this perfection was obviously natural to him. His receptive nature assimilated everything that had gone before him, and, though he remained an Umbrian all his life, he added the characteristics of his own individuality and raised art to a perfection before undreamed of. He was brought up at the court of Guidobaldo of Urbino by his father, who was a poet and painter in this great period of development of classical learning It is thought by some that he studied under Timoteo Viti, but it is known that he was finally a pupil of Pietro Perugino. That which Perugino created,

E. Hautecœur, Phot. Salle VI

1502. St. Michael and the dragon. — Raphael.

Raphael made perfect, and he surpassed his master from the very commencement.

Even in his early works, his genius solved complicated problems. This is apparent in the small picture of "St.

Michael and the Dragon " (No. 1502), in the Long Gallery. The archangel, who has descended from heaven and is crushing the writhing dragon under his foot, brandishes his sword with the right hand. In the background we see a landscape with a burning town, quite after the Umbrian manner. The difficulties in the composition are solved in such a manner that we scarcely suspect them, for it was necessary to give material lightness to the fighting angel, and at the same time a supernatural weight to the body which crushes the monster — elements diametrically opposed. How is this effected? The archangel has been flying through space, and his garments still flutter in the wind. His wings are spread, the body is bent forward, and everything indicates a light and easy flight In contrast to this lightness the dragon writhes under the left foot of St. Michael. By an ingenious artifice, this leg is covered with an iron armour which in itself suggests weight. But it becomes a striking reality when we see the flattening of the body of the dragon. To give us a sense of the size of the dragon another similar monster crouches and approaches. While the leg of the archangel remains immovable in the grasp of the dragon's tail, the upper part of his body is full of movement, and it is this contrast which gives the composition all its strength. The large wings and the white shield lend amplitude to the figure of the archangel who might otherwise appear too small. Although the composition thus shows great originality, the face still suggests the manner of Perugino. It is the type of Perugino's Madonnas, though here inflamed with a holy wrath.

Salle VI

1503. Saint George. — Raphael.

The pendant of the "St. Michael" is the picture of "St. George and the Dragon" (No. 1503). Mounted on a thick-set charger which then represented the ideal of a horse, St. George, in bronze armour, is in mortal combat. The attitude is full of movement and animation, but the horse seems a little unnatural owing to its heavy form. The landscape is simple, yet pleasing.

We notice the Umbrian influences on these works of
Raphael's youth if we compare them with his "St. Sebastian" (No. 1668 A), said on the frame to be of the Umbrian
school.   The landscape, with brown and light grey tones
in the foreground and the long range of blue mountains
in the background, is quite conventional.   The attitude of
the young St. Sebastian is undignified and almost suggests
the movements of a dancer.   The moment the Umbrian
artists abandoned religious subjects and endeavoured to
represent passion they lost all their strength.   It was from
his contact with Florence that Raphael acquired his power
of realism.

Lionardo and Michael Angelo had inaugurated a new
era.   Lionardo taught how to give like values to figures
and the spaces in which they were set.   Michael Angelo,
as sculptor and painter, showed the importance of outline
and muscular development, which was a newly discovered
phenomenon   Raphael, thanks to his incomparable appreciation and sense of the beautiful, impressed a character all
his own on these elements of realism and blended them
with the Umbrian sweetness   It is only the Raphael of the
Florentine period (1504–1508–9) who can have been the
author of "Apollo and Marsyas" (No. 1509).   The god,
lightly leaning on his staff, is listening to the sounds which
Marsyas, seated on a grassy mound, is drawing from his
pipe.   His lyre stands near him on the ground, and a wide
landscape of blue mountains opens out in the background.   There are few works as light and graceful as
this one.   This is not due to the composition alone.
The figures only occupy the sides of the picture, but they
are brought out in relief by their colouring.   The central

part is open and this gives a Florentine character to the landscape without any mixture of Umbrian elements.

E. Hautecœur, Phot.   Salle VI

1509. Apollo and Marsyas. — Attributed to Raphael.

There are points of attraction in the landscape, such as the little white flowers in the foreground, the bushes and trees, the river and a fortress. The landscape is continued in the far distance until we can no longer distinguish anything, but we suspect other vast reaches in the mountains.

These are some of the features of the delicate treatment of the picture. What is still more remarkable is that all the muscles of the two figures are relaxed. The feet of the seated Marsyas seem to touch the ground lightly and the strong muscles of the arms contrast with the light touch of the fingers. Apollo, in a statuesque pose, has freed his left leg from the weight of his body and transferred it to the staff upon which he leans, thus preserving a sense of the laws of gravitation. The expression on Apollo's face is one of attentive judgment, while Marsyas is deeply engaged in his occupation. He is not represented as an ungainly Satyr, but as a young and vigorous peasant. Raphael treated mythological subjects as belonging to our world, — a world, in his mind, surpassing all others in beauty.

It is in this beautiful world that he represented the happiness of maternity as the most charming of all sentiments. We have seen the representation of the Virgin change gradually (perhaps a result of the spirit of the times) from a divine to a more human type. Raphael made this modification perfect.

In "La Belle Jardinière" (No. 1496) we again see a landscape full of variety and detail. The Virgin bends toward the Infant Jesus who stands at her feet and leans against her knee, whilst St. John the Baptist, half kneeling, raises his eyes to the future Saviour in an attitude of veneration. The grouping is strictly correct and is after the manner of the Florentine school. The per-

864   Musée du Louvre — La Belle Jardinière, par Raphaël   Ed. H. phot.

E. Hautecœur, Phot.

Salon Carré

1496.   La belle jardinière. — Raphael.

[129]

sons are close to each other at the expense of the foreshortening of the Child's hand. But that which gives
charm to this work is not so much the skill displayed in
the composition, for the outline is comparatively simple,
as the beauty of the figures. This Virgin, with her fair
hair, is a delicate and tender mother. The Christ is
beautiful and intelligent but childish withal. The expression and attitude of St. John are full of awe, as might
be those of an ordinary child in the presence of a prince.
What Raphael represents here is of this world, but without any ungainly element, and it is because of this attribute in all his work that he is universally understood.
Before this picture we lose sight of model, subject and
composition only to yield to the charm of the *ensemble*.
If there is any peculiar characteristic in his style, it is the
complete harmony which this work exemplifies.

He was the most human of all painters, and this
quality did not suffer when he went to Rome and found
himself in the presence of Michael Angelo.

Here he came in contact with all the noble remains of
antiquity, and we find the echo of the impression which
these things made upon him in "The Virgin of the Blue
Diadem" (No. 1497). This is a purely human scene.
The Virgin bends cautiously toward the Child asleep
on a blue cushion and raises the transparent veil which
covers Him, while St. John the Baptist joins his hands
in adoration. We might also call this picture the Holy
Silence, for everything in it contributes to give an impression of peace. The graceful motion with which the
Virgin raises the veil, the sleeping Child with his little
arms extended, the half open mouth of St. John who

seems to restrain a cry of admiration just as it is about
to pass his lips, the ruins and the landscape in the back-

1497. The Virgin of the blue diadem. — *Raphael.*

ground bathed in mist; all this seems to say: "The fret-
ful world is far away; this is the realm of silence and
peace." But we feel the presence of a foreign element.

The composition is admirably balanced, the outline is firm, but the Virgin's face is strikingly insipid. The colouring, also, in places, lacks strength, as in the garments of the Virgin, and is sometimes glaring, as in the blue of the cushion; the body of St. John, far from being that of a child, has all the vigour and development of an adult. This cannot be due to Raphael's declining powers, for he died in the full maturity of his genius, and we can only infer that a pupil of great talent finished one of his sketches. The Pope and the aristocracy of Rome taxed Raphael's energies to their utmost limit, and, unable to refuse any pressing demand, he often, at that time, made sketches which others finished. Another of these is his sketch of "The Little Holy Family" (No. 1499). On one side we see Jesus kneeling in his cradle and leaning against the Virgin's knee and, on the other side, is St. Elizabeth supporting St. John. This is the work of an artist who is a perfect master of composition. The difference of level between the Child and the Mother is treated with remarkable ease, and the inclined attitude of the Virgin, which causes the balance to be on the right, is counteracted by the marked inclination of her head, so well treated here. There is only one empty space in the composition, namely, that between the heads of the Virgin and St. Elizabeth.

Raphael lays himself open to criticism in his treatment of "The Holy Family of Francis I" (No. 1498). This is a variation of "The Little Holy Family," for it contains the head of an angel between the Virgin and St. Elizabeth, and the composition is richer and more decorative. The vertical is well marked by the person of St. Joseph seated in the background, made necessary by the number and variety of heads and attitudes. The weight of the com-

E. Hautecœur, Phot.   Salon Carré

1498.   The Holy Family of Francis I. — Raphael.

position is in the lower part of the picture, and the angel sprinkling flowers is intended to draw our attention from this. But the pleasure which we derive from this picture is no longer that which the pure beauty of Raphael's art usually gives; the grouping is too cramped, and the reason for the presence of the angel scattering flowers is too obvious. The yellow garments, the reddish-brown faces and the muscles of the children clearly show that, even if the drawing is by Raphael, the execution was left to other hands.

E. Hau.ecœur, Phot.   Salle VI

1500.   St. John the Baptist in the desert. — Raphael.

The same observations apply to "St. Michael Overthrowing Satan" (No. 1504). There is a whole world of evolution between the treatment of the subjects "St. Michael and the Dragon" (No. 1502), in the Long Gallery and "Saint Michael Overthrowing Satan" (No. 1504), in the Salon Carré. The two different treatments are very instructive. In the second, it is the violence of the fall which naturally follows the rapid flight and hurls the dragon to the ground, whereas, in the "St. Michael and the Dragon," it is more the weight of a

E. Hautecœur, Phot.   Salle VI

1513 A.   The Vision of Ezekiel. — Raphael.

heavenly power that we feel. Moreover, the demon in the second picture is thrown down on an incline and struggles with his claws to prevent himself from further sliding, and this natural movement also prevents him from

rising.   But here, even more than in "The Holy Family,"
we notice traces of the hand of a pupil in the expressionless
face of the archangel and in the reddish-brown colour of
the skin.   The folds of the garment have been restored.

E. Hautecœur, Phot.   Salle VI

1506.   Portrait of a young man. — Raphael.

The "St. Margaret" (No. 1501) is quite a wreck, and
we see the hand of Raphael only in the harmony of the
drawing.   It is more than doubtful if we can attribute
the "St. John the Baptist in the Desert" (No. 1500) to
Raphael.   "The Vision of Ezekiel" (No. 1513 A) is a
copy of a picture in the Uffizi Gallery.   The "Portrait

of a Young Man" (No. 1506), representing a young man leaning his face on his hand and supposed to be Raphael himself, does not deserve to be popular, nor can it be attributed to Raphael. The left eye is out of

E. Hautecœur, Phot.   Salle VI

1508.   Portrait of two men. — Raphael.

drawing, and the expression is insipid and wanting in energy.

The "Portrait of Two Men" (No. 1508) has been wrongly attributed to Raphael. It is certainly an excellent work full of strength, colour and expression, and shows an admirable knowledge of movement, but it is marred

E. Hautecœur, Phot.   Salon Carré

1505.   Portrait of Balthazar Castiglione. — Raphael.

by a hardness in the figures absolutely foreign to Raphael.
The creative power of Raphael is again seen in the
"Portrait of Balthasar Castiglione" (No. 1505), also in
the Salon Carré. Here is a witty and distinguished
courtier, an intelligent diplomat and aristocrat. This
work suggests rather than represents character and in-

1507. Portrait of Jeanne of Aragon. — Raphael.

tellect. The treatment is excellent, and the joined hands indicate a man conscious of his worth and of what is due to him. Bright colours are avoided, for they would only have troubled the calm of this harmony.

On the other hand, "The Portrait of Jeanne of Aragon" (No. 1507) is a work representing grandeur and display.

According to Vasari, the sketch of this was made by another artist, and Raphael painted only the head, leaving it to be finished by Giulio Romano. Doubtless this work owes its reputation to the beauty of the model, for this beauty makes us overlook the lack of expression and the dryness and hardness of the colouring even in the face. Criticism has also overestimated the fresco called "The Magliana" (No. 1512), over the door in the Salle des Primitifs, representing the Eternal Father surrounded by seven heads of cherubs. The composition is crowded into too small a frame, and the retouching is too frequent, though the faces are not wanting in charm.

Raphael died of a malignant fever in 1520, at the early age of thirty-seven. None of his assistants or pupils were able to successfully continue his work. Giulio Romano (1492–1546), the most illustrious among them, was of a temperament diametrically opposed to that of Raphael, but he had great richness of imagination and brilliant talent for composition. These gifts he applied to the purely decorative element and, working in an almost mechanical manner, found no opportunity for perfecting himself. He was not insensible to the influence of Michael Angelo, and, as a native of Rome, he could but love the antique. All these different characteristics are united in his works His large "Nativity" (No. 1418) is exquisite in composition, owing to the manner in which the master represents the principal scene between St. John and St. Longinus, and in which the Virgin and St. Joseph kneel near the new-born Child, with the shepherds in the background. But, owing to the influence of Michael

Salle VI

1418.   The Nativity. — Romano.

Angelo, the figures seem larger than life in the setting
in which they are placed. The colouring is harsh,
with yellow shades in the reds and smoky grey in the
whites, and, as with Michael Angelo, the muscles are
strongly marked.

We again find all the qualities of Romano in the "Portrait of a Man" (No. 1422), that is to say, richness of colouring and severity of expression approaching almost to harshness. This picture is clearly by Romano and, for a long time, it passed for a portrait of the master by himself.

Braun, Clement & Cie., Phot.   Salle VI

1420. The Triumph of Titus and Vespasian. — Romano.

The "Venus and Vulcan" (No. 1421), in Salle IX, is doubtless only a copy of a fresco mentioned by Vasari.

"The Triumph of Titus and Vespasian" (No. 1420) shows us how much Romano was beginning to be influenced by the antique. Though the artist strove to keep his works free from the taint of any other influence than that of Raphael, he did not succeed in doing so in his later works, for the influence of Michael Angelo was irresistible.[12]

The creative genius of Michael Angelo was too individual to enable him to found a school, and his imitators, in copying his manner, degenerated into exaggeration. Thus, in the "David and Goliath" (No. 1462)

E. Hautecœur, Phot.   Salle VI

1462. David and Goliath. — Volterra.

by Daniele da Volterra (1509–1566), we see swollen muscles, twisted limbs, and a complete lack of proportion between the figures and the size of the picture. Furthermore, with total lack of taste, this work is painted on marble. Again, Muziano (1530?–1592), in his picture of "Christ and St. Thomas" (No. 1396), endeavours to obtain a maximum of effect. But the manner in which the unbelieving Thomas feels the wounds of Christ is almost brutal.

Sebastiano Luciano, called Sebastiano del Piombo

E. Hautecœur, Phot.   Salle VI

1352.   The Visitation. — Luciano.

(1485–1547), alone of the disciples of Michael Angelo, is
of real importance. In "The Visitation" (No. 1352) the
Virgin and St. Elizabeth salute each other with the
distinction of queens, and their attitudes are full of
dignity; but the figures are too large for the surroundings, and their features are almost too sharp and are

wanting in sweetness. From the point of view of technique, Sebastiano del Piombo was a consummate master, but this work makes no deep impression upon us. Grandeur was a quality unknown to him, and he was unable to approach the dignity of Michael Angelo.

The trio, Lionardo, Raphael, and Michael Angelo, had been preceded in Florence by the trio, Botticelli, Ghirlandajo, and Filippo Lippi. All the efforts of the son of Fra Filippo Lippi left no satisfactory results He was "an ardent struggler, but lacked knowledge and complete mastery of himself." Again, Lippi's pupil, Raffaellino del Garbo (1466–1524), remained a fifteenth century master to the end. His large "Coronation of the Virgin" (No 1303) is full of charm and life, as may be seen in the heads of the angels. There is deep emotion in the expression of the Virgin, and dignity in the figures of the saints, but the composition and colour are of the old school.

Piero di Lorenzo, called Piero di Cosimo (1462–1521 ?), a dreamer and an original, was unable to represent the perfected art which characterised his time. It is still the old manner of grouping and the traditional draping of the garments that we see in his "Coronation of the Virgin" (No. 1416). But Cosimo must have had an individuality all his own Vasari calls him a master of landscape, and this quality we see in two new pictures attributed to him, "The Triumph of Venus" and "The Wedding of Thetis and Peleus" (Nos. 1416 A and 1416 B). In the former, in the midst of a beautiful landscape, Venus, seated in a chariot of shells and surrounded by a numerous suite, approaches the shore. The antique here lives again,

—not the antique read of in books, but that which the
Renaissance imagined. In the other picture we see

1303. Coronation of the Virgin. — Garbo.

Thetis, in a characteristic landscape, led by her father,
Nereus, the old sailor. Peleus, her lover, dressed in the
red costume of a knight, approaches, and bows before

her. All about a troop of gods, satyrs, and centaurs gaily frolic. Hercules is seated in front of a portico of fantastic rocks, and cupids bearing torches accompany

E. Hautecœur, Phot.   Salle VI

1416.   The Coronation of the Virgin. — Lorenzo.

the bride. These two pictures have been attributed by Mr. Berenson to Alunno di Domenico, and he believes them to have been painted about 1490.

Fra Bartolommeo, called Baccio di Porta (1475–1517)

Salle VI

1154.   The mystic marriage of St. Catherine. — Fra Bartolommeo.

seemed destined to develop the principles of architectural
construction in Florence.   He was an ardent admirer of
Savonarola and had the sense of grandeur and of pathos.
The detail in his works is entirely eclipsed by the effect
of the *ensemble*.   In "The Mystic Marriage of St. Catherine" (No. 1154), we are particularly impressed by the
beauty of the drawing and grouping.   The dais on which

the Virgin is seated separates her from the figures at the
sides, and the back of the throne gives her importance.
By her side stands the Infant Jesus presenting the mystic
marriage ring to St. Catherine, whose robe is white, thus
forming a contrast with the predominating dark colours,
and falls in long, simple folds.   On either side of the principal group are saints in different attitudes, and, at the
back, are St. Francis and St. Dominic embracing each
other.   There is in this picture an extreme economy of
space, for, though there is a large number of persons, there
is no impression of overcrowding, perhaps because of the
light tone of the pillars and the fine perspective.   The drawing is also harmonious, as may be seen in the canopy with
its ample and flowing draperies held up by three angels.
The eye, after dwelling on the row of heads, is drawn to
the Virgin in the centre.   Then, passing to the Child, it
follows His extended arm till it drops to St. Catherine
to rest on the folds of her robes.   In the presence of this
original composition, we overlook the fact that the face
of the Virgin is borrowed from Lionardo, and the treatment of the garments from Raphael.

"The Annunciation" (No. 1153), by Fra Bartolommeo,
is constructed on the same lines.   It is not "the humble
mother of the Saviour," but the sublime queen of heaven,
that the angel approaches.   The position of the Virgin is
similar to that just described, and here the saints on the
sides are placed on a different level, thus giving the group
the form of a pyramid.   The foreground, after the manner
of Raphael, is occupied by two young women in strikingly different positions.   The colouring is warm and the
execution delicate, particularly in the modelling of the

articulations where the influence of Michael Angelo is visible The same excellence is seen in the saint holding a sword and in the hands of the Virgin holding a book.

Vasari calls Mariotto Albertinelli (1474–1515) "another Fra Bartolommeo." He was his favourite companion, and certainly approached, but never equalled, the master. In his "Christ Appearing to Mary Magdalene" (No. 1115), we again see the old types. The action is exaggerated and uncertain, and the colouring is too light and has no strength On the other hand, "The Virgin and Child between St. Jerome and St. Zenobius" (No. 1114) is a real work of art. We see here the first attempt at that composition which Raphael later brought to perfection in his "Sistine Madonna" in Dresden The Virgin stands in full face, raised on a pedestal, with the Child in her arms in the act of giving His blessing In contrast to the "Sistine Madonna," the position which Albertinelli gives to the Virgin seems sculptural, and this feature he accentuated by adding the superstructure on which the Virgin is placed He also made her lower her eyes and thus prevented her from seeming to issue from the picture onto the spectator, a danger common to this kind of composition. Her figure stands out in relief against the sky, while St. Jerome and St. Zenobius are less distinct against the landscape and are in profile. The Virgin thus becomes the principal feature of the composition.

The genius of Andrea del Sarto (1486–1531) has quite another character. The problem of construction in his portraits of saints is solved by means of light and colouring. In order to place a great number of persons in a small space, he represents them kneeling and inclined,

E. Hautecœur, Phot   Salle VI

1114.   The Virgin and Child. — Albertinelli.

as in his two pictures representing "The Holy Family"
(Nos. 1515–1516). His drawing is correct; we can see
the articulations in the hands, and the bodies have movement.   In these rich compositions the happy juxtaposition of lights and shades causes these different elements
to be easily distinguished.   We must not look for much

1515.   The Holy Family. — Andrea del Sarto.

character in this artist, for with him sentiment was
never deep, but the hands are cleverly painted and the
flesh is lifelike.   When he attempted grouping, he
failed, as in the "Charity" (No. 1514), in which the
Madonna holds two children in her arms, while another
is asleep at her feet.   This regular pyramid is monoto-

nous, the symmetrical arrangement of the children is devoid of interest, and the face of the Virgin does not show any other expression than the desire to please. Nevertheless, we easily overlook these shortcomings in

E. Hautecœur, Phot.   Salle VI

1514. Charity. — Andrea del Sarto.

view of the beautiful silvery shade of the colouring and the rich landscape so well treated. "The Annunciation" (No. 1517) is a copy of the original in the Pitti Gallery.

Andrea del Sarto had the characteristics of a portrait painter, though "The Portrait of the Advocate Fausti" (No.

1651 A) has more value from the point of view of pose than from that of expression of character.[13]   There is something of the pride of the Medicis in the erect position and in the head thrown a little back.   This energetic man looks up, almost seeming to issue from the frame, and this gives an appearance of intense life to the portrait. There is life also in the warm colouring of the face which is enhanced by the dark garments.

This picture expresses self-confidence and resolution, and forms a strong contrast to the very beautiful "Portrait of a Young Man" (No. 1644), in the Salon Carré, by an unknown master, but which critics now attribute to Francia Bigio (1482–1525), a companion of Andrea del Sarto.   Pain and depression are here depicted in the veiled eye, in the contracted mouth, in the leaning body and in the lassitude of the head.   Francia's life, "without fortune's favour," is here typified.   Many a work of this master, so little known and appreciated during his lifetime, was, after his death, attributed to other artists, and, among them to Raphael.   On close examination it will be seen that this picture has been enlarged, a practice much in vogue in the time of Louis XIV.   It has been to the disadvantage of this picture, for it makes the figure appear too small for its setting

Jacopo Carrucci il Pontormo (1493–1557), a pupil of Andrea del Sarto, was frequently successful, though his "Holy Family" (No. 1240) is detestable in every respect, being hard and out of drawing   On the other hand, he succeeded in "The Visitation," in the outer portico of the Annunziata at Florence   A copy (No. 1242) of this beautiful fresco is in the Louvre and was made by a pupil

1241.   An engraver of precious stones. — Carrucci.

of Pontormo. The grouping and construction are ab-
solutely correct, and the steps serve to vary the level.
The principal group, representing the Virgin and St.
Anne, is triangular. The space is filled with numerous fig-
ures which remind us of Fra Bartolommeo and Raphael.
But it is a harmonious and well thought out work. Pon-

tormo lacked delicacy of execution, as we see in his "Portrait of an Engraver of Precious Stones" (No. 1241), which, however, is a work of some value, for the drawing is firm, the colouring rich, and it gives us an impression of movement in the head. But the features are exaggerated and almost brutal.

Pontormo's pupil, Bronzino, called Agnolo di Cosimo (1502–1572), has treated "The Portrait of a Sculptor" (No. 1184) with much more delicacy. The young artist stands holding a small statue of Venus. The colouring is transparent, and the features are handsome and severe without any exaggeration. The work shows great care, as is seen in the beautiful contrast of the white collar with the black garments, and in the general details of the room. The new picture, "The Holy Family" (No. 1183 A), in the long gallery on the left, shows that Bronzino could paint religious pictures equally well. In the middle, with exquisite golden hair and clothed in a red garment and blue cloak, is the Virgin with the Infant Jesus, to whom St. John offers a piece of fruit. Behind appears St. Joseph as a still vigorous old man, with St. Elizabeth on the other side to give balance to the composition. Although the colouring and atmosphere are excellent, the drawing and grouping are poor.

"The Coronation of the Virgin" (No. 1324), by Ridolfo Ghirlandajo (1483–1561), is a work of his youth, painted in 1503 and, although it has some merit, it is as a whole very insignificant. The colouring is somewhat cold and streaky, and the movements are angular and almost convulsive.

Florence had perfected construction and grouping; and Rome, drawing, outline and proportion. It was left to

E. Hautecœur, Phot. Salle VI

1184. Portrait of a sculptor. — Bronzino.

Venice to perfect colouring. The dawn of this element we
have seen in the first two great Venetian painters, Giovanni
(1428–1518) and Gentile Bellini (1426–1507). It may
be said that the more colour, or rather the love of colour,
predominated with a painter, the more he was likely to
be a Venetian; and the love of colour is always the love
of life.

THE VENETIAN SCHOOL AND CORREGGIO

AT the very beginning of the great Venetian period we find Lorenzo Lotto (1480?–1555). His first work, "St. Jerome in the Desert" (No. 1350), painted in 1500, shows him to have been entirely influenced by Giovanni Bellini and by the art of the fifteenth century. He had no sense of proportion as between figures and landscape, but he had feeling for colour and simplicity. His wanderings in Italy made him sensible to different influences. In a measure, his talent was developed superficially rather than deeply. In "Christ and the Woman Taken in Adultery" (No. 1349), Christ is a Venetian type. Lorenzo Lotto here tried to solve the problem of the luminous qualities of flesh. He also attempted other problems, such as the filling in and economy of space, whence comes this multitude of checkered effects. His figures are full of movement, but everything is absolutely cold, and this is not a good picture, for the crowding of the figures gives a stifling effect. The nobility of action and the expression in the other faces, though a detail, contrast well with the calm attitude and expression of Christ.

Lotto sometimes attained a certain grandeur. "The Holy Family" (No. 1351) is equally good in composition, light, and colouring. By the side of the Child lying on a white cushion, are seated the Virgin and St. Elizabeth, not in an attitude of adoration, but only in that of ad-

158

miration. The Child stretches out its arms to St. John, and, behind the latter, bends an angel under whose large wings two little heads of angels appear. St. Joseph and St. Joachim, bowing reverently, occupy the sides of the picture. The principal group is perfectly triangular;

E. Hautecœur, Phot.   Salle VI

1349.   *Christ and the woman taken in adultery.* — *Lotto.*

the garments spread out on the ground form graceful lines, and the figures on the sides soften the outline of the triangular effect. The heads of the angels under the great wings serve to fill the vacancy above the women's heads and to complete the composition. The luminous and powerful colouring is combined with a distribution of light unknown up to the time of Lotto and first in-

troduced by him. The divine Child is the focus from
which it emanates and it is from Him that a radiance
comes to play upon the head of the Virgin and upon St.
John and the angels, at the same time creating blue
shadows and silvery lights. There is something of the
magic art of Correggio in this beautiful work, and by
such composition Lorenzo Lotto raised himself well above
the then existing Venetian manner.

Giovanni Bellini had taught the Venetian school how
to put a certain charm into the arrangement of figures
on the same plane, and a beautiful treatment in the
movement of heads is found everywhere in this school.
A great sense of joy seems to dwell in these works, such
as, for instance, those of Palma Vecchio (1480–1528).
In his "Annunciation to the Shepherds" (No. 1399), the
Virgin holds the Child to her side, and leans toward the
shepherd who reverently kneels in a charming attitude
of adoration, while St. Joseph looks at him attentively.
Behind the Virgin, before a ruin, kneels the donor of the
picture. The arrangement of the group is simple, but
imposing. The eye rests first on the praying woman,
travels by the head of the Virgin to St. Joseph and falls
to the shepherd on the right. The faces have no very
profound expression of life, and the figures are half ideal
creations of a genial fancy. The attitudes are full of refinement, as, for instance, those of St. Joseph and the
beautiful Venetian. The Virgin herself is a woman of
this world and hardly the mother of God. The whole
is bathed in the warm and golden light of the southern
sun, and the landscape is rich and varied.

Giovanni Bellini had three great pupils — Palma,

Titian and Giorgione. His contemporaries considered
Giorgione (1478–1510) the greatest. They surnamed
him the great Giorgio, or the "divine young man."
There are only three authentic works of his hand in existence, but these allow us to appreciate fully his genius.

E. Hautecœur, Phot.   Salle VI

1399. The Annunciation to the shepherds. — Palma Vecchio.

His quiet power is revealed to us in "A Pastoral Concert" (No. 1136), one of the works in question and to be
found in the Salon Carré. This is not a landscape of
dreamland as were Lionardo's, but a country that we have
all seen without being able to preserve the image of it in
our memories. A warm and soft atmosphere hovers
about it. Under the spreading trees in the distance walks
a shepherd with his flock, the horizon fades into blue
tones and golden shades, and these illumine the tops of
the trees and the uneven ground. In the midst of this

landscape there is a group of musicians consisting of two men, a woman holding a flute, and, to the left, another woman whose position is full of movement. We are afraid

E. Hautecœur, Phot.   Salon Carré

1136.   A pastoral concert. — Giorgione.

of destroying the charm of this creation by attempting to analyse the richness of action in this last figure with the body turned directly toward us, and the left arm stretched across the bosom, while the face is in full profile. The body is soft and lifelike, and the skin is of a brilliant lustre.   The treatment of the colouring is masterly.   The landscape is painted in almost neutral tints and is relieved by the delicate red of the flute player's cloak and by a general velvety tone.   The bodies of the women, suffused with a golden lustre, absorb all the light and appear still more brilliant owing to the neighbouring dark tints.

E. Hautecœur, Phot.   Salle VI

1135.   The Holy Family. — By a pupil of Giorgione.

The mellow light fades away like an echo upon the bright and luminous slopes and fields in the background.

"The Holy Family" (No. 1135), in the Long Gallery, must be considered the work of a pupil or talented imitator who made use of Giorgione's types, as, for instance, in the head of the Virgin.   He must have been a Venetian, a pupil of Giovanni Bellini, and his grouping shows him to have been a contemporary of Palma Vecchio. He also knew how to render character, as is shown in the countenance of the donor, but he lacks the joyousness of Giorgione.   The Virgin is almost sullen, and St.Catherine, whose gesture is conventional, lacks expression.

Giorgione was like a passing meteor. His contemporary, Tiziano Vecelli (1477–1576), a pupil of the Bellinis, was destined to enjoy a continuous life of fame for nearly a century and to exercise a great influence upon following generations.   In presence of the works of Titian, we lose sight of drawing, grouping, and even the subject represented, only to enjoy his marvellous painting which includes all these elements and forms an essentially harmonious whole.   His development was, perhaps, slower than that of Giorgione, as is somewhat indicated by "The Virgin and Child Adored by Saints" (No. 1577).   The rectilinear arrangement of the figures produces a softly undulating line formed by the heads.   The serene beauty of the Virgin recalls the manner of the predecessors of Titian.   She looks tenderly at the Child, while near them an enraptured saint raises his eyes to the group. According to ancient custom a curtain falls behind the Virgin.

In colouring, Titian far surpassed anything that had been done before his time.   His reds shine with a brilliancy and richness which centuries have not been able to dim.   It seems as if the lustre of the colour started from the very base of the coat of paint, and as if there were still more light behind that.   Even the persons in shadow, thanks to the light introduced here and there, attain an incomparable perfection of modelling and intensity of life.

These qualities he developed more and more, particularly in scenes animated with movement and action. "The Virgin of the Rabbit" (No. 1578) is a purely family scene.   St. Catherine is offering the Child to the

Virgin who, with her left hand, caresses a rabbit toward which the Child stretches out his little arms with an expression of keen pleasure Here again the charming purity of outline attracts our notice, but it has now become more energetic It carries the eye from St. Catherine, passes over her head and descends toward the Infant Jesus, to rise again to the Virgin and descend along her arm. But, far from being hard, this line is softened by the curve of the garments and veil and loses itself insensibly in the gracefully draped cloak. The types of the faces already foreshadow those superb, richly clothed Venetian women with luxuriant hair and dark eyes for which Titian afterwards became so famous A warm Italian sky stretches over the beautiful flowering landscape and, in the distance, are green fields and clusters of thick-foliaged trees.

"The Holy Family" (No. 1580), or "The Repast During the Flight," seems to be a variation of this theme. The same harmony prevails here, though it is less delicate. The former picture is remarkable for the continuity of the outline, but, in this one, the outline is interrupted by an empty space which the outstretched hand of St Joseph scarcely fills The undulating outline of St. Catherine rises almost vertically here. St. John is not a child, but a dwarf, and the lamb has the appearance of being made of wood. Notwithstanding the beauty of the landscape, we venture to think that this is the work of an imitator. The same applies to "The Holy Family" (No. 1596) in the La Caze Gallery. But in the other "Holy Family" (No. 1579) we have a genuine work by Titian. With a bold departure from the conventional, the Virgin is placed

1579.   ***The Holy Family.*** — *Titian.*

on the extreme right, thus causing the highest culminating
point of the group to find itself on the side. Her head
is covered with a white veil and stands out in relief
against the dark background. She holds the Child
standing on her lap and bends her head toward St. Agnes
who offers her a palm-leaf. Her eyes fall on the beautiful
saint, who constitutes the real centre of the composition.

This saint is clothed in crimson and green, and her youthful and animated body is full of life Her face is again that of a Venetian beauty. Her hand is placed on the lamb which St. John leads to the Child, thus causing the eye to fall gently, to rise again to the head of St. John. The principal charm of this work is the perfect harmony of drawing and colouring This is to be seen in the faces, the attitudes, the smiling and sunny landscape, and the blue distance which is bathed in a soft and luminous atmosphere.

"The Pilgrims of Emmaus" (No. 1581) is less expressive. Titian has indeed attained a certain degree of realism, but the face of the Saviour is vapid and expressionless. It seems as if the artist had experienced difficulty in covering the canvas, and this is further evidenced by the introduction of the white table-cloth with its clearly defined folds.

The "St. Jerome" (No. 1583) is a study of night effects. The nude body of the saint is painted broadly, with the colour thickly laid on, and stands out distinctly against the wild and romantic landscape. There are a multitude of differently directed lines in this kneeling figure Behind the tall, dark trees is seen the moonlight, magic rays play on the tops of the wild mountains, on the cross and on the crucified Saviour, the light tints of whose body show distinctly in the darkness of the night.

One of Titian's most magnificent creations is "The Entombment" (No. 1584), in the Salon Carré. It was painted in the full maturity of his talent, about 1520, and is one of the most touching works in existence. Beside it "The Entombment" by Raphael seems confused and crowded. In Titian's picture, Nicodemus and St. Joseph of Arimathæa support the body of the Saviour; St. John holds His right arm, and, on the left of the picture, are the Virgin and St. Mary Magdalene weeping. The central group presses round the body of Christ. The principal bearer, Nicodemus, turns his back to us, and Joseph of Arimathæa kneels upon a stone. The type of St. John still vividly, though superficially, recalls Giorgione. The grief here represented is profound. The women are most impressive, and Titian has taken them from life. In the attitude of St. Mary Magdalene, dread and terror at the sight of death are expressed. She is unable to turn away her eyes, and, though she wishes to tear herself away, she looks back as she endeavours to draw the Virgin with her. The expression of despair on the face of the latter, and the convulsive contraction of the fingers, realistically express her grief and her irreparable loss. The modelling of the Saviour's body is admirable. The image of death is not suggested by the face, for Titian has placed it in shadow, but rather by the inertness of the limbs. The left arm falls lifeless, while the right is held up by St. John, and the inanimate hand drops at an acute angle The livid colour of the body is rendered still paler by the deep and rich tones which surround it, while, at the sides of the picture, the colouring becomes lighter. The oblong shape of the picture helps to give a sensation of a forward movement and thus lends to the whole a certain appearance of lightness.

"Christ Being Crowned with Thorns" (No. 1583), in

1584. The Entombment. — Titian.

169

the Salon Carré, was painted when Titian was advanced in
years. The executioners press the crown of thorns upon

Salon Carré

1583.   Christ being crowned with thorns. — Titian.

the Saviour's head by means of long staves. This is a
magnificent work of art, for realism has been boldly
carried to the greatest perfection. There is no grouping

here, but simply a mingling of figures. Christ is a human being whose expression and attitude are touchingly real. His foot is stretched out with a convulsive movement of physical pain, and the colouring of the body is such that one seems to see the coursing of the blood beneath the skin. The whole is broken up by the handling of the light, and yet the details are bound together by it. This light falls in a flood upon the figure of Christ, then on the arms of the executioners and the heads of the Pharisees. There is, in this work, an overwhelming breadth and truth. For a long time the world remained incapable of appreciating such creations, for it did not understand their greatness and considered truth but gross realism.

By the side of this great work, the picture called " Christ on the Way to Calvary " (No. 1582), representing Christ between a soldier and an executioner, appears of less value, although Titian still tried to attain to a complete realism. The body in its white nudity stands out on a dark background, and, in strong contrast, the executioner is placed near the emaciated face.

"The Council of Trent" (No. 1586) is valuable only as a spirited sketch, and its authenticity is questionable. The beautiful picture of "Jupiter and Antiope" (No. 1587) is no more than a ruin, but, in spite of all the retouching, we still feel the charm of the landscape which is one of the most beautiful that Titian painted. We also admire the effect of intense light which the artist, then eighty years old, was able to give to the body of the woman at rest.

No painter, either before or after him, has known

Salon Carré

1590.   Alphonso of Ferrara and Laura Dianti. — Titian.

how to interpret the beauty of woman as well as Titian.
What he represents is very different from the severe Virgin of Botticelli, from the Sphinx of Lionardo, or the sweetness and vapidity of Raphael's women, and is warm and
full of life and its pleasures.   These characteristics appeal
to us in "Alphonso of Ferrara and Laura Dianti" (No.

1590), in the Salon Carré. Alphonso of Ferrara, who plays the part of an attendant presenting Laura Dianti with a mirror, is in the deepest shadow and the light falls only on his forehead. The beautiful woman turns toward the mirror, and, by this movement, her bodice is slightly disarranged. The manner in which she gathers up her hair is full of exquisite grace and it is in presence of these wonderful tresses that we realize what is meant by Titian red The lines of the garment stand out on the dark background, producing a very pleasing effect The arm is charmingly placed in the dim light caused by the folds of the sleeve. In the face, with its dazzling forehead, we feel the blood coursing under the velvety skin and colouring the cheeks. The small, half-closed mouth and brilliant eyes suggest no enigmas; they speak of the joy of living, of happiness and pleasure. In view of so much beauty, it is difficult to take this picture for a portrait. It is an idealized rendering such as the art of the sixteenth century alone could produce, and in it remains a little of that golden age when happiness was a simpler thing than it has become to-day.

In "The Allegory in Honour of Alphonso of Avalos" (No. 1589), the man in armour is a strikingly realistic portrait. A woman is seated with a ball of glass, the symbol of fragile happiness, on her knees. Before her stands Hymen and a cupid crowned with myrtle presents her with his arrows. It is not necessary to know the exact meaning of this allegory. What we admire is the grouping and economy of space, notwithstanding the crowding together of so many figures. This picture shows how great was the mastery of Titian in portrait painting.

We are inclined to think that his " Portrait of Francis I "
(No. 1588) was not painted from life. The full profile
reminds us of a bas-relief or a medal. It is difficult
to become reconciled to the artificial smile on the face.
But the dark pinks of the velvet jerkin are magnificently

E. Hautecœur, Phot.   Salle VI

1589. Allegory in honour of Alphonso of Avalos. — Titian.

reproduced. "The Man with a Glove" (No. 1592), in
the Salon Carré, is a very living portrait. One might
be tempted to say that this picture offers more than
was to be found in the subject of it at any particular
moment, for here Titian gives us all the past and a
little of the future. There is a vague and thoughtful
look in the eyes which are of one who dreams and sees

1588. Francis I. — Titian.

visions. To this face a strong will is lacking, a lack
further indicated by the way in which the body is made
to lean and seek support. The contrast of light and
shade on the face, as well as the fine modelling, is
admirable.

It is probable that the beautiful picture called " The Man

with a Hand on his Hip" (No. 1591) was painted at about the same time as "The Man with a Glove." There is something noble and aristocratic here; the eyes with their look of assurance are full of meaning. The light is beautifully concentrated on a single portion of the face, and the colour-

E. Hautecœur, Phot.   Salon Carré

1592.   The man with a glove. — Titian.

ing is made more striking by the deep shadows contrasting with the white linen.

We are tempted to doubt the authenticity of the " Portrait of a Man" (No. 1593) attributed to Titian. Notwithstanding the fine modelling of the hand, this picture is marred by something strange in the expression. The man does not look us in the eyes. The dark beard, moreover, loses itself in the sombre clothes, and, even if we consider that the hues have blackened with time, Titian, the colourist, could never have painted them even as they must have been originally.

The very fine "Portrait of a Young Man" (No. 1185) in the Long Gallery, must have been inspired by Titian, but executed by his pupil and companion, Giovanni Stefano de Calcar (1510?–1546).

If we combine the grandeur of Titian and Palma Vecchio, allowing only the sensuality and richness to predominate, we obtain the manner of Paris Bordone (1500–1570). His colouring and action are admirable, and he paints luxuriant Venetian hair in the Titian manner, but there is "much flesh and little sentiment" in his pictures. In his "Vertumnius and Pomona" (No. 1178), we see two beautiful but insignificant persons. Pomona seems only conscious of her beauty; it is, however, a pleasure to contemplate the warm life animating these productions

What has just been said applies still more to the new picture by the same artist, "The Portrait of a Woman" (No 1180 A), in the Long Gallery This is a beautiful rendering of a woman with brilliant colouring and charmingly posed Her fair hair contrasts vividly with her deep blue eyes, and the rich tones of her velvet costume throw a delicate reflection over the composition. These qualities exclude all idea of an actual portrait, for they tend to soften and idealize character, as is likewise true of his "Portrait of Jerome Crofft" (No. 1179). This latter is the likeness of a carefully adorned person, but has little life. "Philip II and his Tutor" (No. 1180) also lacks

Salon Carré

1179.   Portrait of Jerome Crofft. — Paris Bordone.

strength and modelling, in spite of the well-executed,
wrinkled face of the old man. There is nothing lifelike about it except the treatment of the old man's hands
and of those of the child.

The "Herodias" (No. 1674 A), though quite in the
manner of Bordone, is, probably, by one of his pupils.

Herodias has almost the same face as Pomona in No.
1178, but the expression of the executioner in shining
armour is brutal and he is badly placed on his legs.
Bordone was not a great artist, but, nevertheless, had decided and definite characteristics.

The same cannot be said of the Bonifazio family.
The three masters of this name, though skilful, were only

E. Hautecœur, Phot.   Salle VI

1172.   The Virgin and Child. — Bonifazio, Veronese II.

imitators. "The Virgin and Child with St. Agnes and St.
Catherine" (No. 1172) is disfigured by archaic attributes.
The attitude of the Child even recalls the old school of
the Bellinis (see No. 1158), and the composition is incoherent. This work may be attributed to a pupil of
Palma Vecchio, owing to the type of the faces. But
"The Virgin and Child with Saints" (No. 1171) brings us
back to the great art of Venice. Here is the rectilineal
grouping of the figures, and undulating and varied lines
formed by their heads. The persons are bound together
artistically, yet the faces, though beautiful, are insipid.

This is the work of an imitator of the Venetian school, probably Bonifazio II Veronese (1494–1555). In a second "Holy Family" (No. 1674 D), which is quite Venetian in composition, a new element is added, namely, the influence of Raphael, which is clearly to be seen in the men's features. The picture full of figures, called "The Resurrection of Lazarus" (No. 1170), is but a variation of Raphael's cartoon called "Feed My Sheep."

Before imitation and the academic manner took root, Venice produced one of the greatest painters of all time, Jacopo Robusti Tintoretto (1519–1594). His contemporaries, though they often praised him, did not entirely understand him. Posterity, owing to the judgment passed upon him by Vasari, was blind to his merits. It was John Ruskin who first recognized his real greatness.

The aim of Tintoretto was to combine the colouring of Titian with the drawing of Michael Angelo, and his talent was so great that these two qualities are united in him in such a manner that we do not notice them separately. Though time has dealt unkindly with his work and so dimmed it that the blues have become black, and it is often only by means of the imagination that we can restore the full splendour of the colouring, enough is left to make us recognize the wonderful power of the master in this respect. Rude restorations have not done less harm than the ravages of time

The charm of light and landscape, the power of movement and the truth of action and expression are all united in his work, as may be seen in the "Susanna after the Bath" (No. 1464). This beautiful woman is seated in the foreground and is being attended by two servants.

The body, still glistening with moisture, stands out in relief against the shadow of the trees. This scene is separated by a wall from the landscape beyond. On the undulating surface of the water some birds float gently, and we perceive two old men near a table in the background. The genius of Tintoretto knew how to avoid

E. Hautecœur, Phot.   Salon Carré

1464.   Susanna after the bath. — Tintoretto.

the danger of the affectation with which this subject was so often treated. Susanna is arranging her hair and this obliges her to turn her head to one side. There is something about her that reminds us of Titian's women. Her occupation and that of her servants cause all the articulations to appear, and her whole body is full of movement. The action of the two attendants is natural and graceful. The two inquisitive old men are half concealed by the table

in the distance and are subordinated so as not to disturb
the poetry of the scene. And yet they are far from being
accessories, for they are drawn into the picture by means of
the handling of the light, which illumines the work with a
single large ray passing over their heads, playing through
the trees and bathing the beautiful woman's body with
a fresh and silvery radiance   If we let our imagination
restore the original deep blue of the water and recall the
soft shadows as they once must have been, we have a
splendid work of incomparable colouring and charm.
All these qualities are wanting in the second interpretation of the same subject (No. 1468), which is certainly not a work by Tintoretto. The expression of
Susanna is meaningless and affected. The two women
on the right with their faces in contact form an unpleasing composition. The different groups do not hold together, and the architecture in the background and the
marble statues in the foreground scarcely suffice to con-
ceal the empty spaces. Neither can "The Virgin and
Child between St. Francis and St. Sebastian" (No. 1469)
be attributed to Tintoretto, for the monotonous attitude
of the saints, the conventional movements of the hands
and, above all, the empty and almost insipid expression
on the face of the kneeling donor of the picture show
the work to be by an inferior hand. But the expressive
sketch of a "Dead Christ with Two Angels" (No. 1464 A)
is certainly by Tintoretto. Death is here interpreted by
a few strokes of the brush in such a manner that the head
falls inertly to one side, while the limbs, owing to the rigidity
of death, are pressed together as they were nailed to the
cross. The tears of the angel are human and touching.

IACOBVS·TENTORETVS·PICT·VENT·OR·IVS

·IPSIVS·F·

Salle XV

1466.   Portrait of Tintoretto. — By himself.

In 1587 it was decided in Venice to decorate the wall
behind the throne of the great Council Hall, with paradise
as a subject.   Tintoretto, at the age of seventy, "prayed
the nobles to give him the commission to paint the paradise which, by the grace of God, he hoped to attain after
death."   It is thus that he created that wonderful work,

the visible interpretation of the immortal conception of Dante.

The small picture "Paradise" (No. 1465) is from the Bevillaqua Palace. From on high a light bursts from the throne of God the Father. Beneath this the Saviour, surrounded by the Apostles, crowns the Virgin as Queen of Heaven. Large banks of clouds succeed each other. In this heaven float the figures of the elect, and in graceful circles and bathed in a magic light, they surround the Divinity seated on the throne above. Innumerable figures emerge from these ethereal clouds, and the rays, starting from the saints, converge toward the central light, as if attracted by God the Father. Light triumphs everywhere, and all sense of weight and every earthly characteristic disappear

Tintoretto was also a great portrait painter. His "Portrait of Himself" (No. 1466), in Salle XV, has a strong and penetrating expression and is a fine work. In his "Portrait of a Venetian Senator" (No. 1471), in the La Caze Gallery, the features are strongly accentuated by the lights which play on the forehead, the nose, and under the eyes, giving them a great intensity of life and modelling the cheeks in shadow. There is the same treatment of diffused light in the "Portrait of a Man with a Handkerchief" (No. 1467). The expression is calm and intelligent, and latent strength is well indicated by the position of the hand. By the side of such works the "Portrait of Pietro Mocenigo" (No. 1470) and the "Portrait of a Man" (No. 1472) appear almost weak in character. They were, probably, painted by pupils, though, perhaps, touched up by the overworked master.

E. Hautecœur, Phot.   Salle I

1471. A Venetian Senator. — Tintoretto.

A genius like Tintoretto could only remain isolated, though Titian and Michael Angelo were his models, and in his works are traces of what Rembrandt was to become.

The family of artists named Bassano attempted to imitate Tintoretto's colouring. Jacopo da Ponte il

Bassano (1510-1592) painted landscapes always constructed on the same model, a blue mountain in the background and groups of trees to the right and left. He was
really an animal painter, but, not caring to acknowledge

1424.   The smiting of the rock. — Bassano.

this limitation, subordinated it by representing Biblical
scenes; hence, "The Entrance of the Animals into the
Ark" (No. 1423), "The Smiting of the Rock" (No. 1424),
and "The Carrying of the Cross" (No. 1426), where the
horses are the most important element. In "The Wedding of Cana" (No. 1425) the personalities are relegated
to the background, while the foreground is principally

occupied by a cat and a dog. As this scene is very unpleasing, we are grateful to the artist for this arrangement.
There is something of the Dutch school apparent in this
Venetian, for "The Grape Gathering" (No. 1428) is quite
in the Dutch manner. His "Descent from the Cross"
(No. 1427), even if not original, is full of remarkable
characteristics from his manner of treating light effects and
grouping. This same may be said of Bassano's son,
Leandro (1558-1623). His "Adoration of the Magi"
(No. 1430) served as a pretext for painting animals in
landscapes similar to those painted by his father

A contemporary of Tintoretto was Paolo Caliari, surnamed Veronese (1528-1588). Though born and educated
in Verona, he held up the mirror to Venetian life. The
zenith of the glory of the republic had been reached and
even passed Innumerable treasures were accumulated
in Venice, and in this great mart, where the East and West
mingled, the politics of the half of Europe were concentrated. The daring navigator, the shrewd merchant, the
astute diplomat became voluptuous in these magic surroundings, and pleasure was raised to the level of an art.
Circumstances made greater expansion impossible, for
the Turkish peril closed the East to Venice. The "Queen
of the Adriatic" now abandoned herself to the enjoyment
of her previously amassed riches. Existence became a
continual vertigo, an unending feast and revelry, and Paul
Veronese was the great interpreter of this life. He had
neither the mystic colouring of Titian nor the grandeur
of Tintoretto, nor did he pretend to much sentiment.
Veronese narrated only, but he narrated with epic breadth.
He represented the Venice of his time and painted hand-

some men satisfied and content with their sensuous life, beautiful women adorned with jewels and clothed in rustling silks, and banquets held in the vast and superb halls of the *Renaissance*.

In "The Burning of Sodom" (No. 1187) are depicted

E. Hautecœur, Phot.   Salle VI

1187.   The burning of Sodom. — *Veronese.*

beautiful women in graceful attitudes.   In the foreground are the two daughters of Lot guided by an angel; behind them, Lot himself accompanied by a second angel; and, against the dark sky of night, stand out groups of trees and the white column of salt.   In the background we see the flames of the city on fire.   Here there is no attempt to express sentiment.   The flight is a pretext for showing the fluttering of robes in the wind and the movement of beautiful arms. One of the fleeing women is tying up her sandal and is thus given a plastic position full of movement and a charming outline.

Paul Veronese, son of a sculptor, had learned art of his father and all his life retained something of the

E. Hautecœur, Phot.   Salle VI

1188.   Susanna and the Elders. — Veronese.

sculptor in his work. When he painted "Susanna and the Elders" (No. 1188), he merely reproduced a beautiful woman of pleasure in a plastic attitude, partially draped in yellow silk. Veronese limited himself to interpreting a gallant adventure in warm colours without appearing to be scandalised, and we can easily understand why all Venice appreciated his work. The "Esther before Ahasuerus" (No. 1189) represents a Venetian court of law. History was doubtless little known to the majority of Venetians, but what Veronese painted they understood. Here is a throne, an idealised Doge surrounded by his council and before him a beautiful woman who falls fainting into the arms of her attendants. The artist did not give himself much trouble in this composition. There are two separate groups, each forming a dazzling and magnificent whole. Guided by his faultless taste, Veronese placed Esther in the back of the principal group. She stands out in relief by reason of her exquisite ivory-pink tints and the brilliant gown. What Veronese created was more dazzling than moving, and this is why he was unable to deal with religious subjects. In "The Saviour Succumbing under the Weight of the Cross" (No. 1194), the assistant executioner is a fine and boldly treated figure. The Saviour is painted in those soft tones and warm colours in which Veronese was a past master. But the faces of Christ and of the two women in the background are without soul. Suffering and human pain were strangers to Veronese. He was a sensual Venetian, and, although he observed all the requirements of the Church, their meaning remained unknown to him. This may be seen in the treatment of his "Calvary" (No. 1195). The picture is bathed in those beautiful fresh tints and silvery tones which might naturally cause Veronese to be called "The Silvery Master." These tones make us overlook many shortcomings, such as the conventional face of the crucified Saviour and the badly composed group which surrounds the Virgin and St. Mary Magdalene at the foot of the cross. The faulty arrangement, as, for instance, the concentration of the whole scene on the left, gives the picture an obvious excess of empty space which is barely filled by the distant view of Jerusalem. The small sketch,

E. Hautecœur, Phot.   Salle VI

1195.   Calvary. — Veronese.

"Jesus healing Peter's Wife's Mother (No. 1191 A) is treated with his usual lack of seriousness. Here are also light-hearted Venetians in a Venetian setting.

Veronese has been called the painter of Venetian banquets, and the description is apt, for no one so well represented the splendours of the "City of Canals." When he painted "The Holy Family" (No. 1191), he

placed the scene in a magnificent palace, with heavy
curtains falling in the background. The Virgin, who
presents the Child to the adoration of the nuns, is a
Venetian type. She has not the captivating beauty of the
Virgins of Palma Vecchio and Titian, but a certain
softness and amplitude of form without character. There
is no sentiment of maternal love indicated in these features. The Venetian woman was a stranger to all intellectual life, for continual contact with the East had
modified her position and made her incapable of strong
emotions. Grace of attitude and movement were, however, second nature to her.

The finest, perhaps, of Veronese's Virgins is the figure
in "The Holy Family" (No. 1190) in the Salon Carré.
In accordance with the traditional manner, the Virgin is
seated in front of a richly decorated curtain which falls,
not vertically, but in softly flowing folds. The Child,
standing on her knees, bends forward and blesses St.
Benedict who is being presented by St Agnes. On the
right St. George approaches. There is no refined psychol-
ogy, no deep feeling, no impressive grandeur here, but
beauty alone and the pleasure of life. The Virgin, a
Venetian patrician with a winsome expression, holds the
Child in a languorously delicate attitude. St. Agnes is
gracefully and most naturally represented, and St. George
bows with the distinction of a nobleman before a lady
of quality. No serious thoughts are inspired by this work.

As we associate the "Monna Lisa" with Lionardo,
"The Sistine Madonna" with Raphael, and "The Last
Judgment" with Michael Angelo, so the name of Paul
Veronese recalls the picture of "The Wedding Feast of

E. Hautecœur, Phot.   Salon Carré

1190.   Holy Family. — *Veronese.*

Cana" (No. 1192) in the Salon Carré.   Here he could
give full play to his talent and be entirely himself.   The
canvas was painted in 1562 for the refectory of St. George
the Greater and is most certainly a faithful representation
of the noisy life of Venice.   It is a painted document.   In
a large *Renaissance* hall, with the Campanile in the background, Christ has just performed the miracle of turning
water into wine.   Seated in the middle of a horseshoe

1192. *The wedding feast of Cana. — Veronese.*

table at the side of the Virgin, He is only faintly distinguished by a feeble halo. The remainder of the scene is entirely worldly. The repast approaches its end, and order is beginning to be disturbed. The children have left their places, and the greyhounds are with difficulty kept in restraint. The servants struggle here and there, loaded with flagons of wine and with dishes. Veronese, apparently, could not help subordinating the fact that he was painting a scene from the Gospels. Our notice is mainly drawn to the principal group on the left, and scarcely rests upon the Saviour. The most interesting figures in this group, which consists entirely of portraits, are the newly married couple; the bridegroom is a portrait of the Duke of Avalos and the beautiful bride is Eleanor of France. Her real husband, Francis I, leans toward his neighbour, and, on the left, is Queen Mary of England. Next to Queen Mary is the characteristic head of Soliman the Magnificent, and beyond him again is Victoria Colonna. The angle of the table is occupied by the Emperor Charles V. The series of portraits continues to our right in the same way. In the middle foreground is Veronese himself playing on the viola; at his side are Tintoretto with a guitar and Bassano with a flute, while Titian holds a bass viol. The tall figure with turban and dagger standing on Veronese's right is Pietro Aretino. On the other side stands Veronese's brother, Benedetto, with a cup in his hand. It is difficult to make out whether he is pledging a toast or is assuring himself of the reality of the miracle.

Thus is this sacred scene converted into a revel. Here again, it is not the construction and composition, which constitute the grandeur of the picture, but the representation of each individual person. Veronese delighted in reproducing a living scene exactly, and this is manifested here with an incomparable richness of movement. Everything indicates the animation of the banquet. Victoria Colonna toys with a toothpick; Avalos takes a cup of wine from the hands of a page; and Soliman listens to what the prince of the Moors says to a servant.

E. Hautecœur, Phot.   Salon Carré

1193.   The repast at the house of Simon. — Veronese.

The whole scene is bathed in the silvery light characteristic of Veronese. Yellow, blue, and red tints are clearly set in juxtaposition, and with these elements of colouring appear purely plastic poses. The servant in the foreground on the right shows a most daring foreshortening, while Benedetto is posing with a studied grace.

Veronese painted this subject over and over again, for every convent wished to possess it for its refectory and his inexhaustible genius was always able to treat it differently. "The Repast at the House of Simon" (No. 1193) was

painted for the Convent of the Servites in Venice.   Here
the guests are distributed at two tables, and, between
them, St. Mary Magdalene is kneeling and anointing the
feet of Christ, while, on the left, Judas rises to rebuke her.
Here again everything is Venetian—the costumes, the
heads, and the high hall supported by columns with is
rich architecture in the background.   The composition,
however, is not without defects.   It is cut in two, and al-

Salle VI

1196.   *The pilgrims of Emmaus.* — *Veronese.*

though St. Mary Magdalene is the principal subject and
is intended to bind the two parts together, owing to
the prostrate attitude in which she almost disappears she
does not fill in the empty space.   The silvery tint, however, which pervades the whole picture makes us overlook
its shortcomings.   Here is no longer the intense life of
"The Wedding Feast of Cana," but a certain gentle and
quieter pleasure is indicated.

This is likewise true of the beautiful picture called " The
Pilgrims of Emmaus" (No. 1196) where Christ, seated
in the middle, blesses the bread and wine.   On the right,

Veronese is standing with his family and his brother Benedetto. One is tempted to say that here, and here only, where Veronese represented himself in the midst of his wife and children, he expressed real feeling. There is a stirring emotion in the expression of Christ and real tenderness in the look which the daughter raises to her mother. If his other works have only stirred our senses, this composition draws him nearer to our hearts.

One might naturally think that these qualities would have made Veronese the greatest portrait painter of Venice. But his special talent was for the handling of throngs of noble men and women. He was not capable of the idealised splendour of Palma, or the depth of Titian. This is evident in the graceful "Portrait of a Young Woman and Child" (No. 1199). It is the likeness of a beautiful woman whose thoughts do not go beyond her toilet and her child, who desires to please and succeeds in doing so.

The second "Portrait of a Young Woman" (No. 1201), attributed to Veronese, should, perhaps, be considered as the work of a pupil on account of the yellow colouring and the rather indistinct features of the face. Also "Christ Holding the Globe of the World" (No. 1200) is so lacking in expression that it, likewise, cannot be considered a work of Veronese. His "Jupiter Hurling a Thunderbolt at Crime" (No. 1198), in the Salon Carré, cannot be appreciated in the position in which it is found at present, for it was intended to decorate the ceiling of the Palace of the Doges and to be seen from below. In this work, however, we discover an influence absolutely foreign to Veronese, namely, the influence of Michael Angelo. The figures are large and exaggerated, and the positions are heavy. It is only God the Father whom Veronese has here represented in his most delicate manner. The same thing may be said of "St. Mark Crowning the Theological Virtues" (No. 1197). What is admirable in these two works is the perfect perspective, the beauti-

Salle VI

1518.   Gaston de Foix. —Savoldo.

ful and brilliant colouring and the elevation of Jupiter and St. Mark in the heavens. This effect Veronese obtained by means of clouds whence he makes figures issue, while, beyond, stretches out a deep blue sky.

While, in Venice, Veronese painted his gay feasts, and Tintoretto his great works full of brilliant colouring, there were some local schools in the neighbourhood of Venice the splendour of which, however, was eclipsed by Venice itself. In Verona flourished Maroni Girolamo dai Libri of whom we have already spoken; at Bergamo were Previtali and Cariani; at Brescia Giovanni Girolamo Savoldo (died after 1548). The "Portrait of Gaston de Foix" (No 1518), by Savoldo, is full of beautiful qualities, and the position of the subject is striking and realistic, with character well interpreted The colouring is rich and beautiful. The two pictures called "Portraits of Saints" (Nos. 1175 and 1176) by Savoldo's compatriot Bonvicino (1498–1555), surnamed Il Moretto, strike us by reason of the beautiful fresh tints, silvery tone of the colouring and the clear treatment of the faces. Giovanni Battista Moroni (1525–1578), a pupil of Savoldo, in the "Portrait of an Old Man" (No. 1395), shows himself a portrait painter of remarkable individuality. There is a conscious and serene intelligence in the wrinkled face, a moral strength acquired in the course of a rude combat with life.

Not far from Verona, in the city of Cremona, a branch of the Venetian school had been founded by Boccaccio Boccaccino (1460–1518). The works of this pupil of Giovanni Bellini show the typical characteristics of the transition from fifteenth to sixteenth century art. "The Holy Family" (No 1168) exhibits careful drawing; the little faces show slight mannerism, but their expressions belong to a fully developed art, while the parallel folds of the drapery recall the past. Bernardino Campi (1522–1592), a member of a family of illustrious painters, continued the development of the school of Cremona, and his "Mater Dolorosa" (No. 1202) proves that this local school was not less subject to the danger of mannerism than were the others.

The sixteenth century was a notable period in the history of art. Ferrara produced Cosmè and Costa of whom we have already spoken, and, at a later period, Dossi and the gentle Benvenuto Tisi da Garofalo (1481–1559). The latter's "Sleeping Infant Jesus" (No. 1353), in Salle IX, is spirited and careful in execution, and the expression of the Virgin reveals great tenderness. A gentle silence reigns in this charming little picture.

But if, to-day, we consider the productions of the school of Ferrara equal to those of Venice and Florence, it is only because of the works of Correggio (1494–1534). He knew well how to interpret the mysteries of beauty and light. We already see indications of his later characteristics in the works of his master, Francesco Bianchi (1447–1510), whose excellent representation of "The Virgin and Child with St Quentin and St. Benedict" (No. 1167) might well be considered a work created by Correggio during his youth. In this charming picture the Virgin is seated on a very high throne placed far in the background. At her feet are two angels with musical instruments, and, on either side, stands a saint. The types of the faces are still those of primitive art, the face of the Virgin bears traces of the Umbrian manner, and the Infant Jesus is stiff in attitude and outline and is quite in the manner of Ferrara. But what is new and surprising is the golden light, which floods the figures and the landscape. The white tints are placed purposely by the side of contrasting colours, and the whole picture heralds the work of Correggio.

Correggio was a master in the production of magic light. He made it radiate from a central point, and his brush

was, as it were, filled with the ardent rays of the sun.
He seized upon all the secrets of flesh tints and fixed

Salle VI

1167.   The Virgin and Child. — Bianchi.

them on canvas.   In presence of his figures of women
suffused with amber light, we feel a mystic charm, a
stirring of the senses.   He combined the delicate shading

of Lionardo with the colouring of Titian. He also shows the powerful drawing of Michael Angelo in his bold foreshortening, yet he always preserves his own charac-

E. Hautecœur, Phot.   Salle IV

1117. The mystic marriage of St. Catherine. — Correggio.

teristics, for all parts of his works are organically bound together and form so many perfect unities.

In the "Mystic Marriage of St. Catherine" (No. 1117), in the Salon Carré, all the light radiates from the Divine

Child and rises toward the faces of the Virgin, St. Catherine and St. Sebastian.   Their countenances are so beau-

E. Hautecœur, Phot.   Salon Carré

1118.   The sleeping Antiope. — Correggio.

tiful that "it seems," says Vasari, "as if they were from Paradise."   With a calm and serene expression, the Child places the ring on the finger of St. Catherine, and this action produces an exquisite grouping of the three hands in close contact, while each remains distinct. The grouping of the persons is quite free and natural, though remarkably varied The Virgin is seated with the Child on her knees, St. Catherine is kneeling and, behind her stands St Sebastian. All this produces a very rich outline. In the background glitters and vibrates a landscape bathed in the transparent atmosphere of a warm sun. This work is, indeed, the union of mystic faith and happy beauty.

Correggio appears to greatest advantage in mythological subjects. In "The Sleeping Antiope" (No. 1118), his brush becomes an enchanted wand. In view of this magic spell, we lose sight of the vigour of the drawing, the boldness of the foreshortening, the grace of the outlines and the artistic grouping of the three figures. A glowing warmth emanates from the body of the woman, and the colours seem borrowed from the sun itself. Her bosom appears to gently rise and fall under the effort of breathing, and there is all the appearance of sleep in the limbs, in the head thrown back, in the raised arm and in the half-opened hand. One feels, rather than sees, the rich undulations of the golden hair. Behind Antiope appears Jupiter in the form of a faun. The spirit of Greece animates this picture, and it is antiquity ignorant of sin which lives again in this work. Strange to say, this great master was unappreciated in his time and died poor and unhappy. When the following generation attempted to imitate him, his mystic light became artificial and the attitudes affected.

DECLINE OF THE ITALIAN RENAISSANCE

AFTER Correggio, with a few notable exceptions, that noble art in Italy which had its first beginnings with Cimabue faded into utter insignificance at the end of the sixteenth century.

Francesco Mazzola, called Il Parmigianino (1504–1540), was born in Palma. His early pictures show a careful study of Correggio's works, but afterwards, in Rome, his manner was profoundly affected by the great masters he studied there, especially Raphael. Of his two "Holy Families," the one (No. 1385) is the development of an idea of Raphael (see Raphael's "Holy Family"); the other (No. 1386) shows decided mannerism. The pose of the Virgin's head is exaggerated, the necks are too long, the pink of the faces has become yellow, there is no life in the body of the woman in adoration, and there is a glaring red on the face of the angel. Federigo Barocci (1528–1602) is still more unpleasant. His large picture, "The Circumcision" (No 1149) is so confused in composition that it is impossible to understand the subject. A vain attempt to imitate the colouring of Correggio gives green and blue shades to the faces, and the red of the garments produces the hard effect of painted porcelain. In "The Virgin in Glory with St. Lucia and St Anthony" (No. 1150), in the Salon Carré, elements of Raphael, Titian, and Correggio are to be found, but the exaggerated ecstasy and the studied effects do not appeal to us.

None of the imitators of Correggio could reproduce his mysterious charm.

Salle VI

1149.   The Circumcision. — Barocci.

And so the great art of Italy began to perish.   Michael Angelo had bewildered and stunned his contemporaries and successors.   Those who now came were but mannerists and only imitated over and over again the same effects. The taste for theatrical action and exagger-

E. Hautecœur, Phot.   Salon Carré

1150.   The Virgin in glory. — Barocci.

ated pathos prevailed everywhere. The ideas of the world had also changed, and to the storm of the Reformation succeeded the Counter-Reformation. The sim-

plicity of the old masters could no longer be appreciated. Extravagant ecstasy, hideous pain, supernatural
rapture and daring colour alone appealed to the masses.

The picture by Cesari (1560–1640), called "Diana and
Actaeon" (No. 1257), in Salle IX, is no more than a
caricature. Diana is an exaggerated repetition of the
Eve of Michael Angelo. Actaeon, in a fury, seems to wish
to destroy everything about him

Mannerism having become unbearable, eclecticism[14]
took its place, and this was an improvement Ludovico,
Agostino, and Annibale Carracci formed an association and founded the first academy of painting, called
the Academia dei Incamminati, whose main object was
the study of the art of the sixteenth century, and the
practice of drawing from models in plaster, from life, or
from still life. Courses in the theory of art and the study
of nature completed the instruction of this system, which,
in its essential features, has been continued by academies
up to the present day, and which we venture to think is
detrimental to originality

The three Carracci themselves were men of considerable
talent, and the best work of their school was what they
themselves did. They made up a remarkably complete
whole. Ludovico found the subject, Agostino arranged
the compositions, and Annibale did the painting.

The best of their combined works are to be found in
Rome and Bologna. Those which show Annibale's (1560–
1609) own peculiar individuality are quite captivating. He
combined various artistic elements with realism in such a
manner that he produced something apparently new. His
"Virgin Appearing to St. Luke and St. Catherine" (No.

1219), in the Salon Carré, was inspired by Correggio. The
Virgin, with the Child in her arms, is enthroned on clouds

1221.   The dead Christ on the knees of the Virgin. — Annibale Carracci.

and is surrounded by angels and saints. Her features are
borrowed from Correggio's women, and, in accordance with
Annibale's treatment, all the light emanates from the Child.

The angels are in the manner of Raphael. In the lower part we see St. Luke with his eyes raised in ecstasy, in contrast to those of St. Catherine who looks down and, at the same time, points to heaven. The construction is strictly pyramidal, an outcome of the Florentine teaching. "The Dead Christ on the Knees of the Virgin" (No. 1221) shows the influence of Michael Angelo, particularly in

E. Hautecœur. Phot.   Salle IX

1218.   The sleeping Infant Jesus. — Annibale Carracci.

the body of the Saviour. Though the action is full of mannerism, as may be seen in St. Francis, and is conventional, as in the Virgin and Mary Magdalene, the faces are full of expression. The treatment of the nude shows careful study, and the arrangement of the numerous bowed figures reveals artistic feeling. "The Virgin of the Cherries" (No. 1217) is absolutely empty and without expression. We are quite unable to understand the popularity of the little picture, "The Sleeping Infant Jesus," in Salle IX, or "The Silence of Carracci" (No. 1218).

The Virgin, with her raised finger, makes a sign to St. John not to touch the sleeping Infant Jesus. The face of the Child is out of drawing, and the expressions are poor. Nevertheless, Annibale Carracci acquired a lasting and well-earned reputation as the father of Italian landscape painting. He, however, did not place himself frankly before nature herself, but only painted parts of what he saw,

E. Hautecœur, Phot.   Salle VI

1233.   The hunt. — Annibale Carracci.

modified according to a certain formula. He composed his landscape, grouped some isolated elements connected with the subject and then skilfully placed his figures. An instance of this we see in his picture called "The Hunt" (No. 1233) in the Long Gallery. Here we see two characteristic and lifelike figures on horseback coming into sight out of a hollow way, and similar qualities are to be found in his other picture, "The Fishing" (No. 1232).

The nephew of Annibale, Antonio (1583–1618), also folowed the traditions of the Academy. "The Deluge"

(No. 1235) with its elongated, contorted nude figures, is a variation of the same subject by Michael Angelo. The man climbing on the left is borrowed from Michael Angelo's famous cartoon the "Soldiers Bathing." In view of this fidelity to its methods, we can well understand that the Academy deplored his death as an irreparable loss. This feeling we cannot share, for a purely

E. Hautecœur, Phot.   Salle VI

1232.   The fishing. — Annibale Carracci.

technical element prevents us from appreciating the works of this period. The preparation of red ochre makes all the dark tints black and likewise renders the light tints hard and glaring.

Guido Reni (1575–1642) is, to-day, the best known of the masters of the school of Bologna. This celebrity he owes to the two half-length pictures called "The Penitent Mary Magdalene" (No. 1448), in Salle IX, and "Ecce Homo" (No. 1447), also in Salle IX. Vulgarised by innumerable chromo-lithographs, they continue to poison taste and kill appreciation for the really beautiful. He himself painted some dozen replicas of them in order to make sufficient money to satisfy his passion for play. The mawkish expression of exaggerated repentance on the face of St. Mary Magdalene and the effeminate Christ,

E. Hautecœur, Phot.   Salle IX

1448.   The penitent Mary Magdalene. — Guido Reni.

both with the uplifted eyes then in vogue, made them easily saleable. The masses took, and still take, the worst kind of affectation for the expression of deep feeling. And yet Guido Reni was an artist of real talent, gifted with rich imagination, an unusual facility for work and great firmness of touch. The pictures representing the legend of "Hercules and Achelaus" (No. 1455), "Hercules and the Serpent" (No. 1457), and "Hercules on the

Salon Carré

1454.   The rape of Dejanira. — Guido Reni.

Funeral Pile" (No. 1453), all in the Salon Carré, are unfortunately particularly noticeable for passionate gestures, limbs outstretched, eyes raised to heaven, swollen muscles and distorted features.

The "Rape of Dejanira by the Centaur Nessus" (No. 1454), in the Salon Carré, shows us Guido Reni in a better manner. The movement of the body of the Centaur is free and light, and there is also freedom of treatment in the outline of the flowing robes. The motion toward the left is well carried out, notwithstanding the movement of Dejanira who turns affectedly on the back of the horse like a circus rider.

At times Guido Reni was subject to the influence of his illustrious contemporary, Caravaggio, the powerful naturalist painter. This influence is noticeable in the "St. Sebastian" (No. 1450), where there are crude lights on the nude torso of the figure, which distinctly bring out the muscles and bones, while deep shadows play on the neck and chest. The face however has again that affected sweetness and the same uplifted eyes. Guido Reni could never free himself from this convention, and David in the "David with the Head of Goliath" (No. 1439) is likewise posed after an entirely conventional method.

Domenico Zampieri, surnamed Il Dominichino (1581–1641), was also a pupil of the Carracci. At the end of the eighteenth and the beginning of the nineteenth centuries, he was considered a demi-god of art in Europe, as the novels of the time bear witness. He is not so affected as Guido Reni and is, therefore, more pleasing. His "St. Cecilia" (No. 1613), notwithstanding the uplifted eyes, has a certain fervour which makes us overlook the expressionless face.

Though a friend of Dominichino, Francesco Albani (1578–1660) leaned rather to the vapid manner of Guido Reni who persecuted him, owing to artistic jealousy.

Albani painted small angels and cupids.   His power does
not go much farther than this, and, from his paintings,

E. Hautecœur, Phot.   Salle VI

1613.   Saint Cecilia. — Dominichino.

we see how happy and prosperous his life must have
been.   In spite of his insignificance, however, he does himself credit in painting little angels.   When, on the other

hand, he attempted small pictures containing many figures, like "Diana and Acteon" (No. 1111), in Salle IX, Albani

Salon Carré

1143.   The protecting saints of the city of Modena. — Guerchino.

became weak and was influenced by the old school, as may be seen in the bowed figure holding a cloak, in the foreground.

What is really unbearable to our modern eyes is the work of a later follower of Carracci's school, Francesco Barbieri (1590–1666), called Il Guerchino. The figures in his picture called "St. Benedict and St. Francis of Assisi" (No. 1142) are ridiculously large; they are twisted and distorted in painful attitudes and make grimaces to express

Braun, Clement & Cie., Phot.   Salon Carré

1538.   A Concert. — Spada.

rapture and ecstasy. "The Resurrection of Lazarus" (No. 1139) is an accumulation of contorted figures and limbs in a crude light, elements due to the influence of Caravaggio. The Saviour has the look of an orator, and there is no trace of real feeling in the picture. In "The Protecting Saints of the City of Modena" (No. 1143), in the Salon Carré, we recognise elements borrowed from Correggio and Raphael, but the composition is overloaded, and the gestures are theatrical. Again, Guerchino gives us another tame and confusedly coloured picture in his "Circe" (No. 1147). As a rule, however, he preferred heavy, dark colours and black shadows.

If Lionello Spada (1576–1622), another pupil of Carracci, was not spoilt by the dangerous influence of the Academy, he owes it to Caravaggio. The "Concert" (No. 1538) has some beautiful and realistic characteristics, and the strong light which bathes the picture is effective.

Of the second generation of the school of Carracci, the colourless and insipid Simone Cantarini (1612–1648), with his two "Holy Families" (Nos. 1207 and 1208), in Salle IX, scarcely deserves mention. The same applies to Andrea Donducci (1575–1655), his senior by many years, author of "Christ and the Virgin Appearing to St. Francis" (No 1271), in Salle IX, and to the landscape painter, Grimaldi (1606–1680), author of the picture called "The Washerwomen" (No. 1327).

The great success of the Bologna academy led to the foundation of a Roman school based on the same principles. Its most important representative is Carlo Maratta (1625–1713), whose manner is empty and superficial, making him dangerous even as a restorer of the frescoes of Raphael. Nevertheless, his portraits are lifelike, as, for instance, the beautiful likeness of "Mary Magdalene Rospigliosi" (No. 1379), in Salle IX, and his portrait of himself (No. 1380) in Salle XV.

Giuseppe Maria Crespi (1665–1747) is a representative of the later academy of Bologna He lacks a knowledge of drawing, paints shadows in uniform brown tones and is influenced by the realistic manner of Caravaggio in his picture called "A School" (No. 1266) in Salle IX.

Giovanni Battista Salvi (1605–1685), called Il Sassoferrato, painted "The Holy Family" (No. 1493) in Salle IX. It is a copy of a picture by Raphael in the National Gallery in London.   It is here that we can best see the

E. Hautecœur, Phot.   Salle IX

1379.   Mary Magdalene Rospigliosi. — Maratta.

artificial mannerism into which art had fallen.   The great art of the sixteenth century was dead, and it was in vain that the eclectics and mannerists endeavoured to breathe a semblance of life into it.   They attempted, by every artifice, to depict expressions of rapture and ecstasy, but all this became vapid sentimentality, and this display of violent gesture, affected treatment of light, and these anatomical tricks, leave us unmoved, because of their total lack of truth.

From all these imitators, often so pitiable, we must distinguish the excellence of Michael Angelo Amerighi de Caravaggio (1569–1609). We do not know who his master was, but his powerful individuality seemed only to recognise one inspiration, Nature herself, and her he knew how to interpret on canvas with consummate mastery. In his life, as in his art, he was bold and uncompromising, and this temperament led to an existence full of change and adventure. Rome, Naples, Malta, and Sicily were the fields of his activity. When he had completed "The Death of the Virgin" (No. 1121) for the Church of the Scala in Trastevere, the monks refused to receive the work, asserting that it was unworthy of the sanctuary. Yet it was a most striking representation of the subject and is a revelation of genius in painting. The Virgin is extended on a couch and is covered with a red garment. The agony of death has caused the body to be rigidly outstretched, The lifeless hand drops heavily from the wrist. A bright, wide ray of tawny light suffuses the calm, dead face and causes black shadows to play upon it, making it the central point of the composition; and this same ray of light binds together the surrounding group. There is nothing artificial here. Every face and every attitude bears the expression of individual grief because each figure is differently treated. In the foreground a woman is overcome by grief, and her tears fall on the white cloth in her hand. One Apostle, bowed with age and sorrow, can no longer restrain his tears and covers

his eyes with his hand.   A second one, on his knees, tries
to master his sobs by holding his hands before his mouth.

E. Hautecœur, Phot.   Salle VI

1121.   Death of the Virgin. — Caravaggio.

And so every head, even those in shadow, is a type; the
Apostles are labourers, of the people.   Grief has rarely
been depicted with so much truth and in so touching a

manner.   It is bitter reality which Caravaggio has placed here before our eyes.

Possessed of so much artistic truth, Caravaggio was destined to be a painter of the customs of his time, as may be seen in "A Concert" (No. 1123) representing a group of nine realistic figures.   They stand before us in a scheme of light which varies from dazzling brilliancy to deep

Braun, Clement & Cie., Phot.   Salle VI

1123.   A Concert. — Caravaggio.

shadow.   The figures are not posing, and each one is rendering his part in his own way.   In the foreground, two of the performers, in full light, are deeply absorbed in their occupation.   Their rapt eyes gaze into the distance, but see nothing.

When Caravaggio represents a "Woman Fortune Teller" (No. 1122) reading the hand of a young soldier, he shows us by the look exchanged between the young man and young woman that they are thinking of a mutual happiness.   To this power of representing character is united a wonderful mastery of the brush. Everything is thrown on the canvas in a broad, vigorous and confident manner. The colouring, particularly in the last picture, shows that some of the gold of the Venetian painters had survived in Caravaggio's art.

E. Hautecœur, Phot.   Salle VI

1122.   A woman fortune-teller. — Caravaggio.

One well understands why the Grand Master of Malta made him Chevalier as a reward for his having painted his portrait (No. 1124). In it we see a proud and self-possessed man solidly set on his feet, his hand gloved in iron and energetically seizing the staff of command. Round the mouth plays an expression indicating intense vitality, and, in his mien, we read a will of iron. There

Braun, Clement & Cie., Phot.   Salle VI

1124.   *Alof of Wignacourt, Grand Master of Malta.* — *Caravaggio.*

was a temperament here resembling Caravaggio's own,
and, for this reason, he was able to interpret it so truth-
fully.

At this period of mannerism and artistic feebleness, a
temperament like that of Caravaggio could not form a

school. His real successor is the Spaniard, Ribera, who eclipsed all the others. Manfredi (1580-1617) only succeeded in imitating gestures from Caravaggio, as is shown in another "Woman Fortune Teller" (No. 1368). He also borrowed Caravaggio's external play of light and a little of his construction, but not his peculiar insight and his power of portraying character. The temperament most resembling Caravaggio's is that of Salvator Rosa (1615-1673) He painted romantic and wild scenes of which one is "A Landscape" (No. 1480). In this we see the creations of a gloomy imagination. We hear the tempest moan in the ravines and see the trees bend under the violence of the wind. In the obscurity we catch sight of some brigands, patches of light, the fire of a carbine and the flash of harness Again, he painted "A Battle" (No. 1479) in a plain surrounded with mountains and brought together a multitude of men and horses before the ruins of an antique temple in the midst of clouds of the smoke of powder; and, notwithstanding all these details, the sureness of his touch makes the whole scene clear.

When Salvator painted a subject picture like "The Apparition of Samuel's Ghost to Saul" (No. 1478) his imagination delighted in the representation of witches and skeletons. A pale light emanates from the phantom's white clothes and plays on the armour of Saul. Saul prostrates himself, before the apparition, and, notwithstanding his attitude of humility, he remains a king in dignity, a happy contrast to his companions, who recoil with terror in the background.

The influence of Caravaggio is also apparent in Do-

menico Feti (1589–1624). The allegory called "Melancholy" (No. 1288) represents a woman on her knees
contemplating a skull. She has the type of Caravaggio's
round-faced women, and a certain freshness of colouring.
Elsewhere Feti united the most dissimilar elements in the

E. Hautecœur, Phot.   Salle VI

1479.   A battle. — Salvator Rosa.

same composition, as in the "Guardian Angel" (No. 1289),
where there is a figure after the manner of Michael Angelo,
though exaggerated, and a vapid head with outstretched
neck. His "Nero" (No. 1286) has swollen muscles and
outstretched arms which seem to issue from the picture
and menace us in a brutal manner.

Michaelangelo Cerquozzi (1602–1660) had the same
characteristics. He was principally a painter of battles
and was surnamed the Michael Angelo of Battles. The
two still-life pictures of fruit (No. 1254 and No. 1255),

in the La Caze Gallery, do not represent him at his best.

Luca Giordano (1632–1705) acquired the doubtful reputation of being, par excellence, a quick worker and, for this reason, was called Fapresto (do quickly). He was a pupil of Ribera and, at times, his imitator. His pictures may

E Hautecœur Phot.   Salle I

1306.   Dance of the Cupids. — Giordano.

be counted by hundreds. He devoted twenty-four hours to painting "The Death of Seneca" (No. 1311) and two days to the execution of other large compositions. Most of his work leaves us indifferent, as "Tarquin and Lucretia" (No. 1310) which is superficial and empty, as are, indeed, all his works. Sometimes, accidentally, he succeeds in producing a pleasing picture like his "Dance of the Cupids" (No. 1306), and one cannot help admiring the richness of his imagination, his excellent decoration and his skill in drawing. All his pictures, except "Mars and Venus" (No. 1305), in Salle IX, are in the La Caze Gallery. "The Dance of the Cupids" is one of his best pictures.

With the approach of the seventeenth century comes an empty period in Italian art. Florence even was no excep-

E. Hautecœur, Phot.   Salle IX

1483. The triumph of David. — Matteo Roselli.

tion. Ludovico Cardi (1559–1613), surnamed Cigoli, tried to substitute eclecticism for the prevailing mannerism. His "Flight into Egypt" (No. 1209), in Salle IX, with its beautiful landscape and strong colouring, is more agreeable than other contemporary productions, for he had not studied Correggio and Paul Veronese in vain. Matteo Roselli (1578–1650) shows himself a complete eclectic in

"The Triumph of David" (No. 1483).   There is a replica
of the picture in the Pitti Palace in Florence.   He had
an appreciation of beauty and of nature.

With Pietro Berrettini da Cortona (1596–1669) we

E. Hautecœur, Phot.   Salle VI

1409.   A concert in Rome. — Panini.

reach "the most empty and unbearable formalism."   In
"The Virgin and Child" (No. 1163) both the Virgin and
Child have the heads of dolls with insipid smiles and
attitudes full of that affected mannerism which was so
long the delight of Europe.   Romanelli (1610–1662) introduced this unpleasing manner into France.   "Venus

and Adonis" (No. 1476), in the La Caze Gallery, is a poor work without expression and scarcely deserves mention.

The eclectics of Genoa are best represented by Valerio Castelli (1625–1659). His "Smiting of the Rock by Moses" (No. 1249), in the La Caze Gallery, shows a certain

E. Hautecœur, Phot.   Salle VI

1408.   The interior of St. Peters. — Panini. .

understanding of grouping and colour and a sufficiently advanced study of the effects of light. Benedetto Castiglione (1616–1670), like Ponte da Bassano, painted biblical scenes, such as "Melchisedec and Abraham" (No. 1250) and "The Expulsion of the Money Changers from the Temple" (No. 1251), merely as a pretext for introducing some charming animal painting, for the faces are without expression and the landscape is purely decorative. Thus

Castiglione is principally attractive in such pictures as his
"Animals and Utensils" (No. 1252), in which he develops
some fine qualities as a colourist.   All his pictures are to
be found in Salle IX.   The characteristic of all this period
of art in Italy is the lack of delicacy of feeling.   In order
to make an effect, the artists exaggerated the action and

E. Hautecœur, Phot.   Salle VI

1574.   Venus and Cupid. — Varotari.

expression, hardened the light and dulled the colours.   It
was a purely superficial and decorative side of painting
which was introduced in order to attract attention, and
this explains why pictures with theatrical decorations
were produced.   The best exponent of this tendency is
Giovanni Paolo Panini (1691–1764), but we must not
judge him by modern standards.   The "Concert in Rome"
(No. 1409) is a picture painted for effect, a work of gala
representation.   The absolute correctness of the perspective is beyond reproach.   We admire the skill of the
drawing in the "Interior of St. Peter's at Rome" (No.

1408). Panini also attempted to give life to enormous surface by means of skilfully scattered groups, or by the play of light which came from without. His two pictures called "Ruins" (Nos. 1411 and 1412) are skilfully executed, but quite devoid of interest. These are in the La Caze Gallery.

Venice, though still under the influence of Titian, Vero-

E. Hautecœur Phot.   Salle VI

1203.   Church of the Madonna della Salute. — Canaletto.

nese, and Correggio, produced a number of decadent artists in the seventeenth and eighteenth centuries. The first is Alessandro Turchi (1582–1648), called Il Orbetto. In "The Death of Cleopatra" (No. 1560), in Salle IX, and in "Samson and Delilah" (No. 1558), in the Long Gallery, the languorous attitudes of the figures show the influence of his illustrious compatriot, Paul Veronese The work is skilful as to grouping and careful in execution, but a little too much finished and artificial in expression.

A poor imitator of Titian is Alessandro Varotari (1590–1650), called Il Padovanino, whose "Venus and Cupid" (No. 1574) seems empty and without life like a thing in porcelain. Francesco Trevisani (1656–1746) displays eclectic mannerism in the "Sleeping Infant Jesus" (No. 1555). Sebastiano Ricci (1660–1734) is a pure mannerist,

E. Hautecœur, Phot.   Salle VI

1328.   Embarking of the Doge on the Bucentaur. — Guardi.

as may be seen in the figures and attitudes of his subjects in the pictures Nos. 1458 to 1461. His pupil, Antonio Pellegrini (1675–1741), in his "Allegory" (No. 1413), once more gives us the expressionless face of a porcelain doll.

Venetian art had not entirely perished, however, for the artistic inheritance was too great. Antonio Canale (1697–1768), called Il Canaletto, painted views of Venice full of atmosphere and light. His "View of the Church of the Madonna della Salute" (No. 1203) is one of the most

beautiful and most characteristic of his productions.   The
sun darts its golden rays upon the cupola of the church,
plays on the water and among the houses, and the vista
along the Grand Canal is executed with boldness and
sureness of touch.   On the piazza there is a gesticulating
and noisy crowd, gondolas float on the blue waters, and
all the external magic of Venice is before us.

Braun, Clement & Cie., Phot.   Salle VI

1332.   Procession of the Doge to the Church of St. Zacharias. — Guardi.

Francesco Guardi (1712–1793) also delighted in the
beauty of his native city.   He charmingly distributed the
light and colour in his picture of "The Embarking of the
Doge on the Bucentaur" (No. 1328).   There is something of the poetry of Venice in this confusion of boats
and in the manner in which the artist causes all the houses
to stand out from the bosom of the waters.   Elsewhere, we
see the movement of a motley crowd in the "Feast Day

on the Piazzetta" (No. 1330); in the solemn "Procession of the Doge to the Church of St. Zacharias" (No. 1332), and in the "Feast Day of Corpus Christi" (No. 1331), in the Piazza di San Marco. Although his execution is, at times, rather sketchy, Guardi, nevertheless, always produces a very original effect. His pictures are painted reproductions of the times of a very personal character and are the

E. Hautecœur, Phot.   Salle VI

1547.   The Last Supper. — Tiepolo.

last representation of the deeds and actions of the dying republic.

Giambattista Tiepolo (1696–1770), by his brilliant colouring, his wealth of imagination, his firmness of touch and facility for work, is the Paul Veronese of the Rococo period. The scene of his picture called "The Last Supper" (No. 1547) is laid within a large and lofty colonnade. The Saviour, indicated by a slight halo, raises His eyes to heaven in ecstasy. Round a long table are grouped the disciples in varied positions and with different expressions of astonishment, fear, rapture and humility. He employed all the wealth of colour to paint the garments, as if he wished to rival Veronese, but he is no servile imitator. He bathes all his pictures in a warm and golden light which here enters in floods and plays on the silk, on the table-covering and on the pavement. His picture No. 1549, consisting of a banner on one side of which are the Virgin and Child with St. John, and on the other St. Martin saying mass, is bathed in a fresh and silvery light, and the grouping, with its two angels who float in the air, is charming.

The great art of Italy was now a thing of the past, but it continued to flourish in Flanders and Spain Tiepolo appeared in an enfeebled generation like a last vestige of the Golden Age. With him, after a long death-agony, the *Renaissance* finally perished in Italy.

THE SPANISH SCHOOL

ALL good art bears the impress of its nationality. The wars of religion had ravaged the East and West for centuries, and Christianity and Mahometanism struggled for the mastery of the world. When the Moors had been overcome, and Christianity had triumphed in Spain, there arose a race of men animated with violent religious zeal, ascetic ardour and devotion to the Church. The long struggle which had just ended brought the natural enthusiasm of these people to its highest point. A reflection of this is found in the art of Spain, notwithstanding the influence of Italy and Flanders.

Luis Morales (1509–1586), called "El Divino," was a very important representative of the Spanish school. He was a painter of sacred subjects, and to the painting of these he was drawn by his strong religious instincts. The figure of "Christ Carrying the Cross" (No. 1707) has a sorrowful expression which is very touching. The head, with its auburn hair, is bowed, and the eyes, heavy with fatigue, only open with difficulty. He walks, but the weight of the cross seems to overpower him. To the intensity of expression and brilliancy of colour is added an execution well worthy of the old masters.

Domenico Teotocopuli, called "El Greco" (1548–1625), was a Greek of fantastic imagination. One would find it difficult to say if his works are the result of exaggeration or of mannerism. In "St. Francis and a Novice" (No.

1729 A) the figures are of inordinate length, have angular limbs, faces of parchment and ashy-grey skin in deep shadow. A picture by El Greco, called a "Portrait of

E. Hautecœur, Phot.   Salle VI

1707. Christ carrying the cross. — Morales.

King Ferdinand of Aragon," has recently been added to the Louvre collection and has no number. There was ardour in the work of this Greek, but he was apparently half mad and repels rather than attracts.

His favourite pupil was Luis Tristan (1586–1640) whose "St. Francis of Assisi" (No. 1730) is a decrepit old man,

1706.   St. Basil dictating his doctrine — Herrera.

strikingly realistic, with an expression of religious ardour
peculiar to the Spanish temperament.

There was artistic feeling in these primitive Spanish
masters though they were unable to give full expression
to it. The exact interpretation of nature was natural to
them, and to this they united religious fanaticism.

Francisco de Herrera (1576–1656), called "El Viejo," was a wild and untamed genius, and there is an almost diabolical cruelty in the "St. Basil Dictating His Doctrine" (No. 1706). We should be tempted to see in this picture a satire against the Inquisition if this idea were compatible with the spirit of the times. "St. Basil, with a book on his knees and in a black cloak, is a bitter fanatic, and the Holy Ghost, who hovers above him, looks like some cruel monster" St. Domenico, on the right, in a white robe, with black lines under his eyes, is the type of a zealot, with ugly and repulsive features from which all human feeling is absent. The whole picture is boldly painted in a vigorous chiaroscuro (the art of judiciously distributing lights and shadows), but, in this case, this is sometimes unequal. It seems as though the flames of an *auto-da-fé* of the Inquisition play upon this picture with their sinister light

Like Herrera, Francisco Zurbaran (1598–1662) was born in Seville He was, par excellence, the painter of monks. These he always knew how to present under a new light, without ever repeating himself, because the subject appealed to him, and the models were always before his eyes His two large pictures of monks, Nos. 1738 and 1739, of which the latter is "The Funeral of a Bishop," are scenes from the life of St Buenaventura. There are in them types which Zurbaran constantly saw in the streets of Seville. He could represent the monk of slender intelligence, but ingenuous heart, as well as the ascetic zealot The draping of the habit always interested him. His colours are well distributed in simple and quiet tones, but he sometimes put in some vigorous

1739. The funeral of a Bishop. — Zurbaran.

and effective touches, such as, for instance, the red Cardinal's hat on the dead body clothed in white.

It was a peculiarity of Spanish art that its representatives were rather developed individually than under the influence of schools. José de Ribera (1588–1656) is an individualist in the strictest sense of the word. Born at

Jativa, a pupil of Ribalta, he found a second home in Naples during the Spanish domination and an artistic model in Caravaggio's works. One may well say that Ribera is the only successor of the great realistic painter Caravaggio, who has inherited all the latter's qualities. He shares with him his personal insight, the gift of finding beauty even in the ungainly, absolute respect for nature, boldness in the use of light, and an imagination which was vivid as well as sometimes cruel. "St. Paul as a Hermit" (No. 1723), praying before the entrance to his cave, is a worn-out, aged man of an almost terrifying realism. The eyes, dimmed by asceticism and age, are fervently raised to heaven. Masses of unkempt hair and a beard encircle the emaciated and wrinkled face. The muscles and veins show plainly, and the crude lights and black shadows make the parchment-like appearance of the skin doubly evident.

"The Entombment" (No. 1722) is poignant and leaves an almost cruel impression. Ribera has here given the appearance of death with great power. On the left, St. Joseph of Arimathaea raises the body. The forearm rests inert, and thus the relaxed articulations of the wrist are made noticeable. The treatment of the limbs gives a vivid impression of death, and we perceive that the works of Michael Angelo were not lost sight of by Ribera. The Virgin appears quite in shadow, and, on one side, St. John wrings his hands in a gesture of grief. In order to emphasize this note of despair and violent emotion, Nicodemus calmly occupies himself with the burial. His cloak throws a bright reflection on the face of St. Joseph, and this brilliant colour contrasts with the livid appearance of the dead body the black shadows of which make it look still more ghostly. Here Ribera is the worthy successor of Caravaggio.

Similar power is lacking in the second treatment of the same subject (No. 1725 A), attributed to Ribera. Here realism is wanting, for death might be taken for pro-

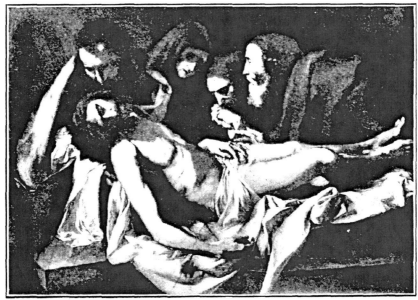

E. Hautecœur, Phot.   Salle VI

1722. The Entombment. — Ribera.

found sleep and St. John is a devoted slave rather than a disciple in great grief.

An attempt has been made to prove that Ribera painted in various manners, but this is not so. He was always the painter of reality. It was with more and more picturesqueness that he learnt how to interpret deep grief and ardent fervour. This we see in "The Adoration of the Shepherds" (No. 1721). He has made the scene quite of this world, without thereby causing it to be trivial. These shepherds, who bow in adoration, are men tanned by the sun and open air. They look upon the Child with melancholy astonishment. They cannot believe in a salvation meant for them also — for them whom happiness seemed to have forgotten in their humble condition. In the background, a young shepherd raising his cap advances timidly, scarcely daring to approach the "Prince of Heaven," and there is quite a study of costumes and manners in these three figures. The Virgin kneels before the Child. She is a beautiful woman of this world, with an expression of earnest devotion, and it is this which makes her superior to her surroundings and which seems to lend her celestial attributes without the assistance of halo or supernatural beauty. The monotonous landscape is bathed in warm sunlight and represents, indeed, "the hard and cruel world which the Saviour came to redeem." "The Virgin and Child" (No 1724) is hardly more than a copy of the central group in the preceding picture. In "The Club Foot" (No. 1725), in the La Caze Gallery, Ribera is a true painter of his time. Here is a mischievous little beggar boy making use of his infirmity to earn his living from day to day, unmindful of the morrow. The close-cropped hair and pointed ears are those of a beggar of the South. To-day, as then, he laughs when he receives charity at our hands, and three centuries have not changed him. The four philosophers, Nos. 1726, 1727, 1728, and 1729, in the La Caze Gallery, attributed to Ribera, cannot be by him, for the workmanship is too crude. They might, perhaps, be ascribed to the rapid painter Giordana.

The works of Ribera are full of truth and reality, but

1721.   The adoration of the shepherds. — Ribera.

the absolutely unrivalled master in these qualities and therefore one of the greatest portrait painters of all time

E. Hautecœur, Phot.   Salle I

1725.   The club-foot. — Ribera.   .

was Don Diego Rodriguez de Silva Velasquez (1599–1680). With the grasp of external attributes, he combined a superior knowledge of character and a remarkable capacity for discovering the innermost workings of the mind and the most intimate characteristics of his models.   He but

too often applied this talent to uncongenial subjects such
as little princesses in the shapeless Spanish costumes of the
times. These works he was obliged to execute for Philip
IV, at whose court he was employed as Master of the
Palace. He treated these insignificant fair dolls, however,
with incomparable skill. In the charming rendering
of the little "Infanta Marguerita Maria" (No. 1731), in
the Salon Carré, we have a child five years of age in a
pale grey dress trimmed with black lace. The right hand
demurely rests on a chair, while the left hangs down
and holds some flowers In this child's rosy round face,
surmounted with tresses of fair hair, glitter two bright eyes,
but there is no look of childish merriment. Velasquez
gave gravity and dignity to this face, and, from her attitude, "this child, with her self-conscious expression
and small closed mouth, is evidently the daughter of a
king " The glistening grey silk dress is stiff, but full of
refinement Velasquez relieved the dull gold colour of
the hair by the delicate shade of the knot which binds it

Still more ungrateful was the task of painting the "Infanta Doña Maria-Theresa (No. 1735), in the La Caze
Gallery, heretofore always supposed to be the wife of
Louis XIV (see foot-note, page 300) The shapeless dress
with the hoopskirt obliges the princess of about twelve
years of age to hold her arms far from the body. She
wears an ugly structure of fair curls. We understand the
repulsion which Louis XIV would have fe't on seeing for
the first time, his fiancée in this apparel. But, notwithstanding all this disfigurement, the manner of treating the
character of this insignificant little person is masterly, and
Velasquez represents her with such truth as to even make

L'INFANTE, MARGVERITE

E. Hautecœur, Phot   Salon Carré

1731.   The Infanta Marguerita Maria. — Velasquez.

her interesting. The genuineness of the "Portrait of a
Young Woman" (No. 1736) has been much called in
question in recent times. Probably it is not an intentional
forgery, but a copy of one of Velasquez' works.

Pliny says that Alexander the Great issued an edict

which forbade any other than Apelles to paint his portrait. Perhaps Philip IV remembered this when he prom-

E. Hautecœur. Phot.   Salle VI

1732. Philip IV in hunting costume. — Velasquez.

ised Velasquez not to allow any other artist to immortalise him. The king, being the most renowned sportsman of his time, was often represented by Velasquez in hunting costume, one example of which may be seen in No. 1732. His expression, in every way insignificant, is not improved by his extraordinarily developed chin, nor by the famous under lip of the Hapsburgs. The position is easy, with the foot slightly advanced; one hand rests on the hip, and a long gun is in the other as he stands in an attitude of expectancy. At his side is his large, intelligent dog. In presence of this picture we can realize how easy it was for Philip IV to become a tool in the hands of his minister, Olivarez. The weakness of the king's nature is but too visible, notwithstanding the eyes with their steady gaze. The treatment of light is most skilful and it illuminates the entire face, models each little detail and plays on his gloves, his clothes and his polished gun. We see the king again in another portrait (No. 1733) in the La Caze Gallery, where he is older and his face is fuller. His age is also noticeable in the looser skin. The eyes look calmly into distance, and are a little more tired and weary, and the mouth is narrower and seems drawn with pain. As with his other models, Velasquez drew from this subject all that was to be found there.

Don Pedro Moscoso de Altamira (No. 1737) is clearly the astute prelate who is better skilled in the things of this world than in those of the next. The manner in which he holds his breviary indicates tenacity of purpose. His well-kept, white and soft hand seems to show his weakness for pleasures. Here is the calm and confident expression of a man who has a goal before him, who pursues it indefatigably and will certainly attain it Strong shadows give the head a very plastic modelling. It is a splendid representation of a remarkable character admirably rendered.

The picture, probably wrongly called "An Assembly of Artists" (No. 1734), is a meeting of thirteen animated persons standing in easy and graceful positions. They are Spanish gentlemen, among whom, on the left, clothed in

E. Hautecœur, Phot.   Salle VI

1737.   Don Pedro Moscoso de Altamira. — Velasquez.

black, is Velasquez himself and also Murillo. They talk with vivacity and gesticulate, without forgetting their natural Spanish dignity of manner. Here, as elsewhere, the artist has composed his picture so naturally and with so little effort that the difficulty of representing and grouping thirteen figures standing in varied positions is in no

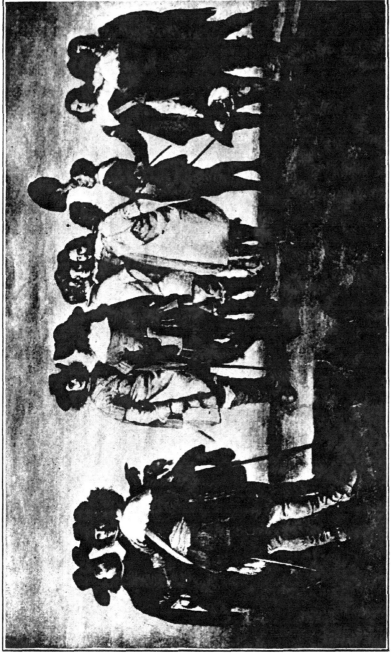

1734. An assembly of artists. — Velasquez.

way apparent. The delicate light colouring of the different costumes is harmoniously and beautifully treated.

This wonderful artist, who lived in the enervating atmosphere of a court, never lost his energy and maintained always the same high level. Jealousy was foreign to his nature. This is why Carreño de Miranda (1614–1685), his successor as court painter, had the good fortune to be protected and encouraged by him. Carreño's "St. Ambrose Distributing Alms" (No. 1702) is agreeable in colouring and careful in execution and clearly shows that he had learned much from Van Dyck and Rubens.

One of Velasquez' greatest titles to admiration as a man was the lively interest which he took in the poor young Bartolomes Esteban Murillo (1617–1682). Born at Seville on the 31st of December, 1617, of very poor parents, Murillo had learned painting with a local celebrity named Juan de Castillo and had learned it badly One of his comrades who had travelled much, brought back to Seville marvellous tales concerning the art of the Netherlands, and, from that moment, the young Murillo determined to travel. His means only allowed him to go as far as Madrid. Then it was that the great Velasquez, with the most absolute disinterestedness, came to his assistance. At the end of two years, in 1645, Murillo returned to his own city. His first large order, namely, eleven scenes from the lives of St. Francis and St. Diego, destined for the Convent of the Franciscans, firmly established his fame. To this series belongs "The Kitchen of the Angels" (No 1716). This picture represents the miracle of St. Diego in a charming and simple manner. The saint, a poor lay brother in an ecstasy of prayer,

E. Hautecœur Phot.

1716.   The kitchen of the angels. — Murillo.

Salle VI

floats in the air with a halo of light surrounding him.
Meanwhile, his earthly duties are performed by angels,
one of whom, in the foreground, is about to fetch water
and is being consulted by a second angel on the subject
of a piece of uncooked meat on which he rests his hand.
One of two charming little angels is cleaning vegetables
and the other is pounding in a mortar, while still another
sets the plates They are surprised in their occupation
by the entrance of a monk followed by the prior and
some courtiers The astonishment of these intruders
is admirably indicated by their attitudes and gestures
The imposible here becomes a reality, and appears
natural. There is in this work all the strength of what
faith can produce, and we are compelled, for a moment,
also to believe in the miracle without question Here we
already see how great Murillo was as a colorist, and that
note of delicate pink, so characteristic in his works, is
found here. The figures of the angels stand out distinctly in the dim light of the kitchen, but they are perhaps a little too scattered, and, thus, the unity of effect
is too much broken up.

When Murillo, at this period, painted a Madonna, as,
for instance, "The Virgin of the Rosary" (No 1712), she
appears in the type of a beautiful Spanish woman with
large dark eyes. She is not the Divine Mother of God,
but only a woman of this world, happy in the possession
of her child and clothed in brilliant colours of red, white,
and green which stand out in relief against a dark background. How tender is the body of this little child and
what natural baby grace there is in the soft limbs and the
gesture of the hands! Murillo, better than any other,

E. Hautecœur, Phot.   Salle VI

1712.   The Virgin of the Rosary. — Murillo.

understood the inmost nature of a child, whether it was a
question of representing the Infant Jesus or a little beggar
boy. "A Little Beggar Boy" (No. 1717), in the Long
Gallery, is a street urchin of Seville who, in a dark corner,
gives himself up to an unæsthetic occupation. A broad
ray of golden light falls on him. The head with close-

cropped hair, and the position make a picture of real life, the life of the South with all its warmth and sunshine. It is one of the numerous enigmas of art that Murillo, who

E. Hautecœur, Phot.   Salle VI

1717.   A little beggar boy. — Murillo.

dared to sound the greatest mysteries, also understood and could render the commonest things of the earth earthy. His faculty for truthful interpretation we see in the two portraits, "The Poet Quevedo" (No. 1718) and the "Duke of Ossuna" (No. 1719), both in the La Caze Gallery. They are living, and this is the greatest praise which can be given to a portrait.

But Murillo is, above all, identified with religious subjects. "The Birth of the Virgin" (No. 1710) is one of
those pictures in which the spiritual and the earthly
appear to be blended in perfect harmony. In the half-
light of a sick-room, a woman of advanced years holds the
new-born child on her knee and smiles at it. One young
woman feels the temperature of the bath with her hand,

E. Hautecœur, Phot.   Salle VI

1710.   The birth of the Virgin. — Murillo.

and another brings the linen. In the background on the
left, appears St. Anne in bed, while near her is St. Joachim, and angels are introduced amongst them in the most
natural manner possible. In the foreground, two little
ones are occupied with the linen basket. What a charm
there is in the way in which one of them turns toward
the dog with a mischievous sign to keep still! Farther
back, are two other persons curiously and reverently
observing the future Mother of God, while, in the air, a
group of tiny angels is fluttering. There is real mysticism

in this union of earth and heaven. A soft ray of light
falls on the bed of St. Anne, but the principal light seems
to emanate from the body of the child. This enhances
the colours of the angels' garments and those of the servants and also emphasises the brilliancy of this blending

E. Hautecœur, Phot.   Salle VI

1708.   The Immaculate Conception. — Murillo.

of tender pink and pale yellow. As a contrast to the
celestial light, we see the pale glow of a fireplace well
back on the right.

An artist animated by so sincere and simple a faith was
predestined to become the painter of that great mystery
of the Immaculate Conception. Murillo painted this subject more than thirty times, and it is by these works that
we can best judge his religious enthusiasm. One of the
first of the representations of this subject (No. 1708)
shows the Virgin standing in the crescent of the moon.

The head is inclined, the hands are joined, she is the servant of the Lord receiving the mystic grace, and there is humility in the features of this beautiful countenance surrounded by angels. Murillo's pictures had not here lost all earthly attributes, for below, on the extreme left, are worshippers with admirably rendered characteristics. One of them, in ecstasy, raises his eyes to the Divine apparition, and, on the features of a second, suppressed wonder is depicted. A boy contemplates the holy form with awe and astonishment, while an aged man, probably the donor of the picture, is apparently explaining the mystery to him. The whole is painted in warm, golden tones, as with the light of setting suns.

From the next picture (No. 1709) all earthly elements are banished. The Virgin, with her eyes raised to heaven, is no longer a woman; she is a divine apparition. Around her are angels in adoration, filled with joy at the ineffable grace received by her and, through her, transmitted to all humanity. Heaven is open, and from it descend streams of light which surround the Virgin. The silvery crescent of the moon shines with magic brilliancy, and the clouds throw dazzling reflections on the blue and white of the Virgin's robe. Far beneath is the earth in deep darkness.

Another work with the same qualities is "The Holy Family" (No. 1713), a representation of the Trinity. The features of St Elizabeth, so full of character and dignified by age, are idealized by deep feeling St. John offers the cross to the Infant Jesus who is standing on the knees of the Virgin. Her embrace is close and natural, and the look which she raises to the Divine Child conveys everything of tenderness and adoration of which the heart is capable. The attributes of heaven once more ap-

E. Hautecœur, Phot.   Salle VI

1709.   *The Immaculate Conception.* — *Murillo.*

pear, for it is open, and in it the Holy Ghost is seen, and God the Father borne on the clouds blesses his well-beloved Son. It is impossible to describe the mysterious quality of the light, the beauty of the bright bodies issuing from the environing shadow and the tender harmony of colour.

Braun, Clement & Cie., Phot.   Salle VI

1704.   Guillemardet, French Embassador to Spain. — Goya.

The two pictures Nos. 1714 and 1715 suffer from the coldness of the marble on which they were painted.

As compared with Velasquez and Murillo, the remaining

representatives of Spanish art are of relatively small importance. The "Burning Bush" (No. 1703), by Francisco Collantes (1599–1656), is a landscape of ideal composition, but without any personal character. The brown

L. Hautecœur, Phot. Salle VI

1704 A. A young Spanish woman. — Goya.

tones are after the manner of the Italian school. In a still life picture of " Fruits and Musical Instruments " (No. 1720), Antonio Pereda (1599–1669) shows himself to be a careful but insignificant artist. Juan de Arellano (1614–1676) in his picture of " Flowers " (No. 1701), the colours of which are confused, does not offer us much of interest.

However, almost a hundred years later, Spain produced

another painter of importance to all art, Francisco Goya (1746–1828), who, at a period when classic convention-

E. Hautecœur, Phot.   Salle VI

1705.   A young Spanish woman with a fan. — Goya.

ality and affectation of attitudes had invaded central Europe, created works full of life and satire. They are masterpieces executed in a vein of caricature. He has put something of his sarcasm into the picture called "F Guillemardet, Ambassador of the French Republic to Spain" (No 1704). Here is a man who owes his elevation to the Revolution, and who, even as an Excellency, feels himself superior to his rank The position of the body gives a picturesque and very rich effect As a true Spaniard, Goya loved warm hues and enlivens the dark clothes with tricoloured plumes and a scarf

The portrait of a "Young Spanish Woman" (No. 1704 A) is a truthful rendering of a southern girl The grey tones in the folds of the dress and in the fan are remarkable. It is a speaking work of art

Equally spirited is the treatment of a "Young Spanish Woman with a Fan" (No. 1705), in a black mantilla, and with a pink knot in her hair as an adornment. The erect pose, almost inclined backward, and the crossed arms are full of Spanish grace. The soft pearl grey background of the picture not only gives brilliancy to the colouring, but blends the whole into harmony. A recent acquisition is the portrait of Don Evaristo Perez de Castro (No 1705 A).

Much has been said concerning the true aim of art, and many have thought that its object was to give pleasure only; but as Mr. Pater says, "Art comes to you professing frankly to give nothing but the highest quality to your moments as they pass, and simply for those moments' sake."

NOTES

PAGE 27

(1) The very fine picture "St John the Baptist" (No. 1274) was originally ascribed to Uccello, but this is undoubtedly incorrect Signor Ventieri attributes it to Bianchi Ferrari and Mr Berenson to Piero di Cosimo. So this work, we must confess, represents a still unsolved problem.

PAGE 29

(2) It is difficult to recognize in this picture the manner of Fra Filippo, but, in view of Vasari's statement that the head of the Madonna is a portrait of Lucrezia Buti, one feels inclined to think that Lippi must have been the author of it.

PAGE 33

(3) This picture has been ascribed, and very justly, to the School of Pesellino

PAGE 39

(4) Attributed to Jacopo da Sellajo by Makowsky

PAGE 44

(5) Attributed to Amico di Sandro, that is to say, to the School of Botticelli by Mr. Berenson.

PAGE 64

(6) Attributed to Raffaelino dei Carli by Mr Berenson.

PAGE 66

(7) These pictures, as well as Nos. 1571 and 1572, were attributed by Crowe and Cavalcaselle to Pinturicchio.

PAGE 75

(8) This picture is, perhaps, not entirely from the brush of Giovanni. It was attributed to Rondanelli by Crowe and Cavalcaselle.

PAGE 85

(9) Herr Thove attributes it to Correggio in his prime.

PAGE 88

(10) This picture was attributed to the School of Costa by Crowe and Cavalcaselle.

PAGE 91

(11) Signor Venturi ascribes the very fine female portrait, No. 1573, to Costa, but we must feel that its authorship is still a problem.

PAGE 143

(12) "The Circumcision" (No 1438), wrongly attributed on the frame to Bagnocavallo, is undoubtedly by Giulio Romano, according to Morelli.

PAGE 154

(13) This work is not from the brush of Sarto, but is a work of his school

PAGE 209

(14) Eclecticism, in this sense, was a term applied to a school of artists who endeavored to select and imitate only the best characteristics and most salient features of all the schools which had gone before.

INDEX OF PAINTINGS

INDEX OF PAINTINGS

UNKNOWN MASTERS OF THE ITALIAN SCHOOL

FOURTEENTH CENTURY
1620. The Virgin and Child S VII
1621. The Virgin surrounded by angels and saints.
S VII.
1622 The crucifixion S. VII
1623 The coronation of the Virgin. S VII.

END OF FOURTEENTH CENTURY
1624 St Jerome S. VII.
1625. St Peter and St Paul S VII

FIFTEENTH CENTURY.
1628. Vittorino di Feltre S VII.
1629. Pietro Apponio Salles des Dessins.
1630 Dante. S VII.
1631 St. Jerome. S VI.
1632. St Augustine. S. VII.
1633. St. Thomas Aquinas. S. VII.

SPANISH SCHOOL

* It has been discovered recently that No 1735 is not a portrait of Doña Maria
Theresa, but of Queen Maria Anna.

INDEX OF ARTISTS

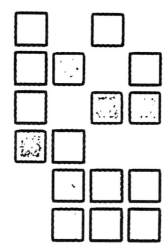